The Story of
Yone Noguchi

The Story of Yone Noguchi

Yone Noguchi

MINT EDITIONS

The Story of Yone Noguchi was first published in 1915.

This edition published by Mint Editions 2021.

ISBN 9781513282510 | E-ISBN 9781513287539

Published by Mint Editions®

 **MINT
EDITIONS**

minteditionbooks.com

Publishing Director: Jennifer Newens
Design & Production: Rachel Lopez Metzger
Project Manager: Micaela Clark
Typesetting: Westchester Publishing Services

To
HIFUMI, MY DAUGHTER
SIX YEARS OLD

Contents

I

How I Learned English

My first sensation, when I got a Wilson's spelling-book in my tenth year, was something I cannot easily forget; I felt the same sensation when, eight years later, I first looked upon the threatening vastness of the ocean upon my embarking on an American liner, where I felt an uneasiness of mind akin to pain for the conquest of which I doubted my little power. I remember how I slept every night with that spelling-book by my pillow, hoping to repeat the lesson whenever I awoke at midnight; the smell of the foreign book, which troubles my nostrils I feel even today when I think about it, charmed, mystified, and frightened my childish mind. My teacher, in fact the only one teacher in the whole town (Tsushima in Owari province), who knew anything of English, soon found his inability to advance beyond the twentieth page of the book; when I got another teacher, who had been newly appointed to the grammar school of the town, I was asked to buy a copy of Wilson's First Reader, which my father got at Nagoya after walking fifteen miles. It happened that one day I lost the Reader; when it was discovered some months later, it was in the little shrine of the Goddess of Mercy at the corner of the Kojoji Temple yard where I used to wrestle with other boys after school was over; doubtless I had placed it there offhand when I hurried to the sport. As I had only got the book after causing great trouble to my father, I could not tell him about its disappearance; but as I could not study my lesson without the book, I borrowed one from my friend who studied with the same teacher, and copied whole pages in the storehouse, where I trembled when I heard father's steps. From the winter of my eleventh year, the English Readers began to be officially taught in our school; and we were put under a far better teacher, whom the town engaged for his English; but we boys soon grew suspicious of his knowledge, which we had thought wonderful at the beginning, when one day an American missionary (the first foreigner I ever saw) called at our school, and our English teacher seemed not to understand his words.

The school was in a certain Buddhist temple long left to dusts and ruin, the prayer-hall of which, with a huge gold Buddha idol on the sacred dais, was temporarily turned into our classroom; my unusual love of pranks often drove me to climb up that Buddha's shoulders, and once I wrote down on his holy breast the words, "See the boy and the dog," with white chalk, for which I was at once punished by the teacher. We were one morning frightened by the sudden fall of the Buddha, when the house shook terribly from *jishin* (earthquake); for some reason I could not run away to the open yard; and as a paper *shoji* door fell over me to make my little head immovable through its wooden frame, I shut my eyes, and cried hard for help. When the shaking was over, our English teacher told us that *jishin* was "earthquake" in English; that word was the longest word I learned in those days. My eldest brother at Tokyo sent me a copy of somebody's geography for a New Year's gift, which I took around among my friends to impress their minds that I was quite superior to them; in fact, such a book was a great curiosity then in our town. I know I must have been very ambitious to learn the English language; whenever my father sent me on an errand without, I always carried the Reader in my sleeve; once, on my way to somewhere, I wrote down with chalk my English lesson on all the wooden fences I came across. Father scorned me for my delay when I returned; on my confession of what I had done, I was sent out again to rub off with wet rags what I had written.

I left the town, a dreamy valley with another name, the Town of Purple Waves, in my thirteenth year, for Nagoya, where I became a student at the Otani school, newly opened, under the support of the main Buddhist temple of the Otani sect. It was here that I had my first foreign teacher, who used Longmans' Readers for textbooks. How he looked I do not remember today; but the strange smell of his skin or breath from too much tobacco smoking, the smell we Japanese used to called Western-people smell, is most distinctly in my memory. And another thing I remember about that foreign teacher is that he had a little anchor tattooed on his wrist. Although we were a little suspicious of his blue mark, we never knew that he was only a common sort of sailor, till he was seen at a show acting as umpire of a wrestling match between an American sailor and one professional Japanese wrestler, when he was dismissed from school. In those days, when we had little experience with foreigners, a white skin and red hair were a sufficient passport for a Western teacher in any Japanese school. My ambition to learn English was never satisfied with only the textbooks; I found a man whom I took for a scholar from the mere fact that he had recently returned from America (I had hardly any knowledge of America then beyond my little imagination, in which all the Americans lived in marble houses), and took him Smiles's *Self Help*, which I had heard of in those days. How my hope was overthrown when his English was discovered to be limited to the names of wines and drinks which he had learned at a certain down-cellar in San Francisco as a barkeeper! Receiving a note from my brother that my school would be changed for a better one, where I could get a thorough education under a far more competent teacher, I moved to the Nagoya High School under a prefectural governor's supervision; I was given here the Second National Reader, which was far too easy for my mind, which intended even then to go over every page of the English dictionary to put it in my memory. It was my ambition to make my study advance in the shortest time possible, so that I could understand what a foreigner spoke. How often, hoping to hear the English words for the test of my ears, I stood at evening against the fence of a missionary's house as if in my poem which I wrote the other day:

> "I put my face against the bolted door, bare, desolate;
> Beyond the door, I know, lies the lonely, the invisible,
> the vast (or is it the Eternal?)."

Once I saw in the street a Western woman with a little girl, whom I followed, again with the same purpose, that is, to test my ears to find whether I could understand their words; I followed after them still further in despair of catching them. The girl suddenly turned back and shouted: "Mamma, what does this fellow want?" I ran away from them at once in great shame; but I slept well that night, I remember, from satisfaction that I could at least understand what the girl said.

I came up to Tokyo, not waiting for father's permission, in February when I was fourteen years old, as my boyish ambition had grown too big to be peaceful in a provincial city. The first English book I ever read in a Tokyo school was Macaulay's *Life of Lord Clive*, the beautiful style of which excited my adventurous enthusiasm. When my weakness in mathematics made me think it quite difficult to pass the Government's examination, I left the school in a sort of preparatory system for Keio Gijiku founded by Fukusawa, the greatest educator modern Japan ever produced, the school where today, twenty-four years later, I turn my morning steps to deliver the so-called lecture—of the real worth of which I have my confessed doubt—on English poetry. At this Keio I was put to learn somebody's economy and history; and you will wonder to know that I learned also Spencer's *Education* (why *Education* for a small boy to be educated?), to which I clung as if, in an old story, a blind man to a huge elephant. And it was here also that I became acquainted with Longfellow's village blacksmith, who looked

> ". . . *the whole world in the face,*
> *For he owes not any man.*"

I grew now even to despise the spoken English language since my first touch with the imaginative literature; I often excused myself from the conversation class under an American teacher, and forgot how hours passed in the pages of Irving's *Sketch Book,* which made me long for England and Westminster Abbey. One day I picked up at a second-hand shop Gray's book of poems and Goldsmith's *The Deserted Village,* which, both of them, I even determined to translate into Japanese at the same time; is there anything under the sun hard to accomplish for a boy?

Now came a sudden turning of my life's page; I was thrown, of course of my own free will, into the strange streets of San Francisco in the month of December of 1893, in my eighteenth year; my first despair there was my linguistic incompetency, which made me mad even to curse over the Japanese teachers who had not given me the right pronunciation of even one word. I used to carry paper and pencil, when I had to go out on some business, and write down what I wanted to say; I was often taken for a deaf mute. Indeed if I had stayed as such, in the years of my Western life, with my thought in the golden silence whose other name is meditation, I might have become ten times wiser. From the immediate necessity of bread and butter (I had not known it before), and also because I thought it a right opportunity for learning the spoken English, I found a job as a kitchen boy in a certain Jewish family; I started at once to bother the Irish cook with each name of the things I found in the kitchen. When I was almost through with the things there, I took a further step to learn the strange names in the dining-room and parlour, the first sight of which, I distinctly remember, took my breath away. That Jew must have been rich. Although I knew that my being in the family was through my service as a boy, my young head was deep in my English study; from want of my hands' certainty (perhaps that of my mind) I do not know how many dishes I broke. It was about that time that I came across Kingsley's *Three Fishermen,* and tried to remember it so that I could recite it at any odd moment. One morning the cook (that hot-tempered Irishwoman whose heart must have been dancing as Yeats' fairies) asked me to get a dozen eggs at the grocer's near by; while carrying in my hand the paper bag of eggs from the grocer, I kept up reciting *The Three Fishermen* so that I quite forgot the part of my hand and dropped the bag to the pavement. I was bitterly scolded by the lady of the house when I got back, and told that the price of the broken eggs would be taken out of my wages. In the family there was a young lady attractive enough to remind me of Scott's Rebecca (I was somehow familiar with *Ivanhoe* already then), who taught me the Third California State Reader every evening in my little down-cellar room. My great sensitiveness to female beauty, which was in a speedy way of development, made me restless rather than learn the lesson in face of this beautiful woman, whose rich hair, when she sat by me, almost touched my blushing face. But that was sweet indeed. The one I hated with a sense of fear was the master of the house, large and stout in physique, red-faced again with a wonderful red nose. He came down to the cellar every morning calling me John, and pushed out his foot for his shoe to be cleaned. The feeling of being something like a slave made me rebel; besides, when I was told that I had to work one whole week for nothing as I had broken one large window, I decided to excuse myself from the house, not troubling to ask for my release, under the dusk of the night. When I left the Jew's house, I put myself at a Japanese newspaper office in the city, where I was engaged as a carrier boy. I was glad with the new place, because I found there a whole set of the *Encyclopædia Britannica.* From my childhood days I had not minded walking; while walking to deliver the paper to some eighty places (we had a circulation of less than one hundred and fifty in the city), I always thought about some English book; and when I came to a lonely street with nobody in sight, I was pleased to recite loudly the lines from my memory. Hamlet's soliloquy I was thinking the greatest English writing; how hard I tried to remember each line of it. There lived at the office five or six young Japanese; to cook pancakes with water for their breakfast was my morning work. One day when I was perfectly forgetful of the burning pancakes on the fire, as my whole mind was absorbed in this newly discovered rôle of Hamlet, my young friend called me by name; in a fit of anger I threw over him a big tin pan brimming with flour and water. His dirty clothing was miserably white-washed. When I repented of my rash conduct, I found that we had to go without breakfast that day; and worse still, my poor friend had no other dress to change to. I was obliged to offer him my clothes when he had to go out, and to stay in bed myself the whole afternoon, now thinking on the reality that foolishness was altogether too expensive for me, then on Napoleon, who, as I had read somewhere, had one suit of clothes between him and his brother in his younger days.

When I set out to peddle the cheap modern Japanese colour-prints which some Japanese had put down at a certain boarding-house in pawn for his board, to gain practice in spoken English or brush away my Oriental shyness in speech was the first purpose before earning a little pocket-money; I remember that my first day's clear profit amounted to almost two dollars. But the colour-prints were soon exhausted; and I turned my mind next to canvassing for advertisements in our paper, from which I received but little success. One day when I was walking lazily with no particular purpose I found a little second-hand bookshop in a certain street, and dropped in to look around at the books, among which my quick eye caught a book *Dora Thorne,* a story translated in Japan by the now Viscount Suematsu under the title of *Tanima no Himeyuri* or the "Lily of the Valley." I felt a sudden desire for its possession which, being almost irresistible, made me commit the first and last crime of stealing; I put the book under my coat while the proprietor, an old man who seemed quite scholarlike and sympathetic, was looking away. I was so sorry for such a shameful act when I returned home; and my sorrow grew larger when my mind, I dare say of considerable literary taste at least for my age, found the book did not encourage my soul's curiosity. I decided to take it back to the shop and to apologise to the old man for my crime; and I took the book one day there. But my courage failed, and besides, I could not find a chance to see the man alone. So I took it there again a day or two later; and the man approached me from within, when seeing me, and cast a friendly smile from his open and honest face, a type I only saw among the Americans of older generation. Then he asked what book I liked. "I cannot say what I like, but I know what I do not like; and here is one of the books not to my taste," I exclaimed. And to astonish him, I made my confession about the book as best I could. How glad the old man was to hear my story. He wanted to express his forgiveness emphatically when he asked me if I wished to take some book or books to read. I was glad that my crime was forgiven in a really nice way, and more glad that I gained a good friend from whom I could draw out the books to read. He handed me Keats' book of poems, when I told him that I wished to have a book which should have more an inner beauty than Longfellow; and he said that if I read the book intelligently, I might feel

> "... like some watcher of the skies
> When a new planet swims into his ken."

This old bookshop keeper and I became quite friends during my long stay in California; it was he who was the first to congratulate me when my first book of poems, *Seen and Unseen*, made some little literary excitement in America. He wished me the most sincere godspeed at my departure, a few years later, for New York, and still farther for London. I had a secret hope on my way home to Japan, in 1904, to find him again in San Francisco; my disappointment was that I could not see any shadow of his little shop or himself in all the city.

My stay at Palo Alto, a college town, whither I went by walking from San Francisco as I felt I heard the voice of a scholarly call, is one of the sweetest memories of my life. I found my home there in a certain lawyer's house, whose chief attraction for me was that it contained a library. There I first put my fingers on the pages of a book of Hugo's while the whole family were absent. The lady of the house, and her daughter, both of them, used to attend Stanford University, the mother for the study of zoology and the daughter as a literature student. The family had quite a sympathy with myself; when the lady discovered my great love of books, she did not mind if I read a book even while picking the strawberries. She often built a fire herself when I over-slept from my reading so late at night. Although I did not believe in the reading of newspapers it seems that my mind grew from those days attracted to them; and I soon found that to understand the newspaper writing was another study. When the China-Japan War broke out, I was working as a dish-washer at a country hotel in the next town to this Palo Alto; the chef was a Japanese, who from his ignorance of English prized me highly, as I served him with all the news translated. "Now you might go upstairs and read the paper. Come down after one hour with the news of victory," he used to say. At the beginning I could not understand the paper well; but after a month of hard study with a dictionary (I rarely went to sleep before one o'clock in those days) I made myself sufficiently able to understand the news at one reading. When the war advanced, and my purse grew heavy with my earnings, my restless mind again asked for a change; and my first desire was to see my old friends at the paper office in San Francisco and talk on the war, so I hastened back there again, where the proprietor begged me to stay with him, this time not as a carrier boy but as a translator. I thought it rather interesting, as I was deadly tired with my experience as a servant; during three months I stayed with the paper—in fact, I translated everything from the American papers, from the Japanese Emperor's Imperial Edict to a tragedy of a street girl. I was not yet fully twenty years old; but it was I who ran *Soko Shimbun*, our Japanese paper, even for a short while. I think that it was in those days of the China-Japan War that I had more chances to speak English; to anybody I came across, I tried to explain the difference between China and Japan, and above all, why we won the fight. A certain Mr. Creelman lectured here on the so-called Port Arthur brutality, on his way to New York from the war field at Manchuria. On the night of his lecture, I appeared with my protest, which I had all ready to deliver against that lecturer on the spot, if my courage had not failed. The vogue of the *Mikado* or the *Geisha*, a comic opera, at that time made my true Japanese heart pained, as I thought it was a blasphemy against Japan; how often I wished to shout from the pit or gallery on its absurdity. To play a patriot or an exile was one of my pleasures at that time.

I took only Poe's book of poems with me when I left San Francisco in the month of April 1896, for Joaquin Miller's hillside home, back of Oakland, the "Heights" as he called the place. My leaving the city to which I had returned only five or six months before, should be put partly to the count of my restlessness of mind, but the chief reason was in my thought that books should be read slowly but thoroughly after having a good sound rest. Although I read quite many books for my age, particularly for a boy of foreign origin, I thought that I could not say that I did well understand them; it is true to say that I never read thoroughly all the words, from the first to the last page, of any book of them. The fine sleeping which had hitherto been denied to me since my arrival in America, I really thought was the first necessity for the good understanding of books. When I selected Poe's poems, I meant that I would try to study his poetry alone at Miller's garden where, as in *To Helen*, the moon shed her light on the roses:

> "*That gave out, in return for the love light,*
> *Their odorous souls in an ecstatic death.*"

I read each line and all the words of Poe's poems, my first love being *Annabel Lee;* in time they grew almost chiselled in my mind, as I could recite them and bring out their separate words for my need; at the highest moment of my Poe saturation, I confess, I felt I was a Poe myself, and could not speak any other language but Poe's; I even thought that I might be his incarnation when I wrote the following, the second English writing of my life, for instance:

> *"Mystic spring of vapour;*
> *Opiate odour of colour;*
> *Alas—I'm not all of me!*
> *Wanton fragrance, dewy, dim,*
> *Curls out from my drowsy soul;*
> *Wrapping mists about its breast.*
> *I dwell alone,*
> *Like one-eyed star,*
> *In frightened, darksome willow threads,*
> *In world of moan.*
> *My soul is stagnant dawn—*
> *Dawn, alas, dawn in my soul!*
> *Ah, dawn—close-fringed curtain*
> *Of night is stealing up; God—*
> *Demon—light—*
> *Darkness—Oh!*
> *Desert of No-More I want;*
> *World of silence, bodiless sadness tenanted;*
> *Stillness."*

When the poem (being printed in a little magazine, as my existence already excited some curiosity then) was criticised as a plagiarism from Poe's *Eulalie,* which contains the exact following words:

> *"I dwelt alone*
> *In a world of moan,*
> *And my soul was a stagnant tide."*

I wrote an open letter in a San Francisco paper that I was glad for having the moment when I felt the same thought with Poe, and I could not understand why I could not say the same thing if I wanted to say it; and I declared I should like to understand poetry from the point that it would be a journal of one's feeling or the footmark of one's soul's experience. As I had a poor vocabulary and almost no technique of composition, I started, from the beginning, to cultivate my inner feeling, and to express as best I could under the command; I had even moments when I felt thankful for my lack of visible beauty in technique, as my ideal poet, from the first, was one such as I wrote of in *The Pilgrimage*, my fourth book of poems:

> *"He feels a touch beyond word,*
> *He reads the silence's sigh,*
> *And prays before his own soul and destiny:*
> *He is a pseudonym of the universal consciousness,*
> *A person lonesome from concentration."*

I soon grew to forget my Poe mania, when my inner sense of poetry or poetical individuality seemed to be developing from my naked lying before the Great Nature. How I read the heart of Nature, and also my soul, "separated from the mother, far away, abandoned by his native land and Time," alone in the "dream-muffled canyon," in love with "Being-formed Nothing," you may read in my *Seen and Unseen*, the first book of poems published in December of 1896, from a San Francisco press.

Thus my first period of learning the English language ended with this simultaneous entering of my first stage of English writing; but I have no hesitation to say that the books were often my sweet companions as when I led the so-called tramp life in the three succeeding years, once alone travelling in the Yosemite Valley, where I took Milton's book of poems, whose organ melody did well match the valley's rhapsodic grandeur. On the other occasion when I walked down from San Francisco to Los Angeles (how I walked those hundreds of miles impresses my present mind as quite wonderful), I was constantly with Shelley, who is the poet bound naturally to come after Keats. I found on my arrival in Los Angeles that my copy of Shelley had been lost; from my immediate desire to get another copy, I engaged to work one week at a wooden-box factory; when I had worked well those seven days, I was able to buy, besides the Shelley book, Verlaine's book of poems, which appeared in an English translation first at that time. Ever since he is one of my beloved poets. The first impression that I received from that French poet, I should say, awoke in my mind fifteen years later by

Enkakuji Temple of Kamakura, where I wrote the following as the end of my poem, *Moon Night:*

> *"Down the tide of the sweet night*
> *(O the ecstasy's gentle rise!)*
> *The birds, flowers and trees*
> *Are glad at once to fall*
> *Into Oblivion's ruin white."*

During the four years that I stayed at Miller's mountain home, I learned more names of English writers and poets and more of their writings, I think, by Miller's accidental talk on them, than in any previous four years, which made me wish to acquaint myself with their works. Often I left the "Heights" for San Francisco to read the books at the city library. It was Miller who initiated me in Thoreau and Whitman. While at San Francisco, sometimes I stayed at a Japanese boarding-house where I was charged nothing, as I made a service of English letter-writing for the proprietor, and sometimes at a certain William Street, one of the most insignificant of little alleys, where my Japanese friends published a comic weekly; here at the latter place, I happened to become an actor in a farce which set the whole town to laughing under the heading "How a Japanese Poet helped a Burglar." One afternoon I was reading a book in the room which was a parlour and sleeping-room and editorial office by turns (we occupied the lower floor, the upstairs rooms were occupied by a Spanish tailor who happened to be out that afternoon) when I became a burglar or thief from my stupidity. A young boy, Spanish or Mexican, about the same age as myself, knocked at my door asking for the key which, he said, might fit the rooms upstairs; it was his intention, he declared, to move the things away by the command of the tailor who had engaged some other house. "I lost the key on my way here," he said. How could my mind of innocence doubt him? I helped him to open the upstairs rooms, and also assisted to move down a few things of some importance; when I found that it was too much to carry them by himself, I offered him my service to help him at least with the large looking-glass. We walked some seven or eight blocks when we were pursued by a large fat Irish policeman, who took us by force to a police station and duly locked us up. The next day I made the first and last public speech of my foreign life to clear myself from the charge. I believe that my little speech was a masterpiece, in which I said that it was a case of Japanese etiquette or humanity turned to crime in America by wrong application. It was my last speech; and I hope that so it may remain.

I left California for New York as the stepping-stone to old smoky London. In New York, where my first attempt to sell my poetical wares and my California fame as a poet of two or three years back seemed quite nicely forgotten, I decided to play a sad young poet whose fate was to die in a garret. Nature here did not appeal to me much; and when life grew more interesting to study and speculate on, I again took up my reading of English books with renewed interest. I found a little job in a certain family to wash dishes in the morning and tend the furnace of a winter evening; here I used all my hours for reading the books which I drew freely from the library near by. It was in those days that I read through the whole set of Turgenieff and some parts of Tolstoi; before Turgenieff, Daudet was my favourite author. But I did not forget to read the books of poems; and I wrote a few poems which I published in my first London book, *From the Eastern Sea.* I was glad that, when my English knowledge, however little it might have been, and my inspiration played together most harmoniously, I could turn out something as follows:

> *"'Twas morn;*
> *I felt the whiteness of her brow*
> *Over my face; I raised my eyes and saw*
> *The breezes passing on dewy feet.*
>
> *'Twas noon;*
> *Her slightly trembling lips of passion*
> *I saw, I felt; but where she smiled*
> *Were only yellow flashes of sunlight.*
>
> *'Twas eve;*
> *The velvet shadows of her hair enfolded me;*
> *I eagerly stretched my hand to grasp her,*
> *But touched the darkness of eve.*
>
> *'Twas night;*
> *I heard her eloquent violet eyes*
> *Whispering love, but from the heaven*
> *Gazed down the stars in gathering tears."*

II

Some Stories of my Western Life

I

MY NEW LIFE BEGAN WHEN I left Tokyo for California; on the 3rd of November, 1893, my friends saw me off at Shimbashi Station. I felt most ambitious when they wished me godspeed; but my heart soon broke down when my eldest brother, who came to Yokohama to bid me a final farewell, left me alone on the *Belgic*. That was the name of my steamer, an almost unimaginably small affair for a Pacific liner, being only three thousand tons. I cried when the last bell went ringing round to make the people leave the ship; I cried more when my brother became invisible among the hurrying crowd and distance; it was my most bitter experience, as I cannot forget the pain of sadness of that moment even today. I stood by an iron rail on the deck, a boy only eighteen years old, alone, friendless, with less than one hundred dollars in my pocket. I immediately grew conscious of the fact that I had to face unknown America, a land of angels or devils, the darkness.

It is true that it was my first experience to see such a vastness of water, as I was born in a place out of sight of the sea; and its restless motion made me at once recall my sickness on the water which I had experienced when I joined a fishing party on the river Kiso several years before. The most unagreeable smell that filled the "Chinese steerage" made me already ill, even before the engine began to turn; I was practically thrown in as if a little bundle of merchandise for America. I could not eat, drink, for many days, and I vomited even what I did not eat, when the ship rolled. I was often obliged to tie me round the iron pole by my canvas bed; I soon became a thorough sea-hater, as I am still today.

The steamer duly reached San Francisco on a certain Sunday morning; we, I and a few other fellow-passengers, were taken to the Cosmopolitan Hotel, whose shabby appearance looked then palace-like and most wonderful. And within it was not less handsome. The American room was the first thing for us; even the sheets and the soft pillow, quite strange for the head acquainted only with hard wood, were a novelty. We put all the fruits we had bought (what splendid California fruits!) in a white bowl under the washing table; when we were told, to our utmost shame, that that bowl was for another purpose, we at once thought that we were, indeed, in a country alien in custom, and had a thousand things to study. We acted even more barbarously at the dinner-table; we took salt for sugar, and declared the cheese to be something rotten. We did not know which hand, left or right, had to hold a knife; we used a tablespoon for sipping the coffee, in which we did not know enough to drop a lump of sugar; we could not understand that those lumps were sugar. I stepped alone out of the hotel into a street and crowd; what attracted my immediate attention, which soon became admiration, was the American women. "What lovely complexions, what delightfully quick steps," I exclaimed. They were a perfect revelation of freedom and new beauty for my Japanese eye, having no relation whatever with any form of convention with which I was acquainted at home; it is not strange to say that I could not distinguish their ages, old or young; they appeared equally young, beautiful, even divine, because my discrimination lost its power at once. True, it took some months, though not one year, before I could venture to be critical toward their beauty; for some long time they only looked, all of them, perfectly-raised California poppies. I am happy to say that my first impression never betrayed me during my eleven years of American life; not only in California, but in any other place, they were my admiration and delight.

Now to return to the adventure of my first day in San Francisco. I again stepped out of the hotel after supper, and walked up and down, turned right, and again left, till the night was growing late. When I felt quite doubtful about my way back to the hotel, I was standing before a certain show window (I believe it was on Market Street), the beauty of which doubtless surprised me; I was suddenly struck by a hard hand from behind, and found a large, red-faced fellow, somewhat smiling in scorn, who, seeing my face, exclaimed, "Hello, Jap!" I was terribly indignant to be addressed in such a fashion; my indignation increased when he ran away, after spitting on my face. I recalled my friend, who said that I should have such a determination as if I were entering among enemies; I thrilled from fear with the uncertainty and even the darkness of my future. I could not find the way to my hotel, when I felt everything grow sad at once; in fact, nearly all the houses looked alike. Nobody seemed to understand my English, in the ability of which I trusted; many of the people coldly passed by even when I tried to speak.

YONE NOGUCHI

I almost cried, when I found one Japanese, fortunately; he, after hearing my trouble, exclaimed in laughter: "You are standing right before your hotel, my friend!"

My bed at the hotel was too soft; it even imitated, I fancied, the motion of the sea, the very thought of which made me sleepless. I sat alone on the shaky bed through the silence of midnight, thinking how I should begin my new life in this foreign country. In my heart of hearts, I even acknowledged my dead mistake in coming to America.

I had one introductory letter to Mr. Den Sugawara, of the Aikoku Domei, or "Patriot Union," a political league, whose principal object was to reform the bureaucracy at home, to speak more directly, to put an end to the Government of the Satsuma and Choshu Clans, by demonstration with the publication of free speech. I called on him next evening at the back of O'Farrell Street; the house, this Aikoku Domei, was wooden and dirty. I really wondered at the style of Japanese living in San Francisco; I cannot forget my first impression of the house where I made my call. It reminded me, I thought then, of something I had read about the Russian anarchists; I confess that my feeling was gloomy. The narrow pathway led me to the house of two stories; the lamplight from within made the general aspect still worse. I climbed up the steps which could not be wholly trusted; when I entered within, I smelled at once fishes and even Japanese *saké;* the clapping hands and noisy chattering from another room made me quite inquisitive. I presented my letter to the said Sugawara, an office boy to a certain doctor in those days, one of the prominent members of Parliament today; and was soon admitted into the room of discussion. My boyish blood, with love of adventure and romance, began to rise when I found out that the people, most of them young and dauntless, were discussing how to help the Hawaiian kingdom. I looked round the room over each face of the people; and was arrested by a face of different race, swarthy and large, doubtless a Kanaka, who was, I immediately found out, no other than Mr. Robert Wilcox, the Hawaiian patriot. I had already read about him a good deal; but I had never dreamed I should see him within a few steps. When the talk came to a close, it was decided that three members of the Aikoku Domei should return home for advocating the independence of the Sandwich Islands; to live in history as a Japanese La Fayette was no small matter at all. I contributed all the money I could spare (every cent I gladly parted with) on the spot for the Hawaiian cause and her Majesty Queen Lilliokauani; it was partly from my little vanity not to be taken for a mere boy, but one worthy to be taken account of. Vanity is always expensive.

The League was then publishing a daily paper called the *Soko Shimbun* or the *San Francisco News,* for which I was engaged as a carrier; the paper had only a circulation of not over two hundred. I did not enter into any talk about payment; I soon discovered it was perfectly useless when we hardly knew how to get dinner every day. You can imagine how difficult it was for five or six people to make a living out of a circulation of two hundred; I believe it was Mr. Crocker's kindness (the house belonged to him) that we could stay there without regular payment of rent. When he decided to put up new houses, he only begged us to move away, not saying anything about the payment. By turns, we used to get up and build a fire and prepare big pancakes, you understand, with no egg or milk, just with water. And a cupful of coffee was all we had for our breakfast. When we had no money to make supper, we often went to a Chinese restaurant on Dupont Street, or somewhere, to eat for the payment of his advertisement in our paper. "Oh, such a life," I exclaimed, finding it unbearable at the beginning; but I became soon satisfied, even glad, as I could have plenty of time for my own reading. I assure you that I was quite a reader, and proud of my being advanced in my taste with literature, particularly poetry.

There was no bed in the house; we used to sleep upon a large table, a mass of newspapers serving as mattresses. I took down a volume of the *Encyclopædia Britannica,* which, I am sure, contained Macaulay's essay on Byron; I made a nightly habit of reading it before I went to sleep, using the book as my pillow. Lord Byron was my favourite in those days, as with any other boy; that was long before my days of Keats and Shelley. There was a man called Watari, who acted toward me rather fatherly; it was one of my delights to talk with him, more often listen to him, every morning, while still in bed, on poetry and politics; I cannot forget how he tired me with his Darwinism, which I little understand even today. It was about that time I began, little by little, to read *Hamlet;* once I decided to remember every word of his famous soliloquy, and having my mind fully occupied with the recitation of it, I forgot for some time to leave my best wishes with the papers which I had to hand in to Japanese readers at each place.

There was another club or league, mainly social, but not less political, called the Enseisha, or "Expedition Club," which always acted differently from our Aikoku Domei, and often expressed even open enmity toward us. Truth to say, we had not one day when we did not fight in the papers. Enseisha was then publishing its own daily (the *Golden Gate News*), which was not better off financially than our paper. And not only with pen, our hands, too, helped to settle our troubles; when we called its members cowards, they gave us the name of liars. And we got still more angry. I can say, when I reflect on the Japanese life in San Francisco seventeen years ago, that we had at least one pride, not to move from commercial motives; we never thought about money and fortune. Really, I was surprised to observe such a great change in the general aspect of Japanese life when I stopped in San Francisco on my way home in 1904; it made me rather sad to know that money was the reigning power. It was regarded as foolish, even harmful, to talk on politics, which was the only one subject for the Japanese of the old days. A great fight suddenly ensued between the Aikoku Domei and Enseisha from the suspicion that two members of the former were connected with the dirty work of Tanaka, who robbed in one way or another the money of Japanese labourers in Idaho while he was their manager; we tried to prove the probity of our friends, while the others blackened us. It was when we held an open debate to explain the whole affair at St. George Hall, Market Street, in January of 1894, that one of my dear friends in those days, Terutake Hinata, beat a member of the Enseisha in the hall, who attempted to disturb the meeting, and wounded him with an iron bar, which he hid under his coat; as a consequence he was arrested. It took some time before a peaceful settlement was brought about between the two parties. Mr. Hinata is today one of the figures in the Japanese Parliament. Whenever I see him, we talk on the old days in California, and sigh in reminiscent mood from the feeling of sadness mingled with a sort of joy which only belongs to the memory of a younger day.

When I began to reflect on what I had come to America for, to ask myself how far my English had improved, and what American life I had seen, I regretted my mistake in associating with the Aikoku Domei, and put an advertisement as a "schoolboy" in the *Chronicle,* following the way of many other Japanese boys. What domestic work has that "school-boy" to do? The work is slight, since the wages are little—one dollar and a half a week. We have to leave our bed before six, and build a fire for breakfast. Don't throw in too much coal, mind you; your Mrs. Smith or Mrs. Brown will be displeased with you, surely. She can hear every noise you make in the kitchen, she can see how lazy you are as clear as can be, no matter if she be busy with her hair upstairs. "Charlie, isn't the water boiling?" she will cry down. Charlie! Your father didn't give the name to you, did he? A great pile of dirty dishes will welcome you from the sink when you return from your school about four o'clock. Immediately, a basketful of peas will be ready to be shelled. You must go without dessert, if you eat the strawberries too often while picking. Saturday was our terror-day. We had to work all day beginning with the bathroom. Your lady will let her finger go over the furniture when you finish. "See!" she will show you her finger marked with dust. Patience! What a mighty lesson for the youth! You must not forget to wash your stockings before you go to bed, and hang them on a chair. How could we afford two pair of stockings in our schoolboy days? What a farce we enacted in our first encounter with an American family! Even a stove was a mystery to us. One of my friends endeavoured to make a fire by burning the kindling in the oven. Another one was on the point of blowing out the gaslight. One fellow terrified the lady when he began to take off his shoes, and even his trousers, before scrubbing the floor. It is true, however fantastic it may sound. It was natural enough for him, since he regarded his American clothes as a huge luxury. Poor fellow! He was afraid he might spoil them. I rushed into my Madam's toilet-room without knocking. The American woman took it good-naturedly, as it happened. She pitied our ignorance, but without any touch of sarcasm. Japanese civilisation, if it was born in America, certainly was born in her household—in some well-to-do San Francisco family, rather than in Yale or Harvard.

The work of "schoolboy," which I took up with much enthusiasm, served for some time as a delightful break in my American life; but its monotony soon became unbearable, and I decided to go on foot to Palo Alto, as I thought (as in a Japanese proverb, "The children who live by the temple learn how to read a sutra") I might learn something there. I slipped out of my employer's house one early morning from the window, as I was afraid the lady would not let me go if I asked my wages. When I reached the Stanford University ground, it was near evening; I called at the house of Prof. G——, where my friend was working while he attended the lecture courses. I was permitted to stay with him till I found some way to support myself. Through the kindness of the wife of Prof. G—— I got a job at Mrs. C——'s to work morning and evening, and by turns I found a place at the Manzanita Hall (a sort of preparatory school for Stanford), where I was admitted to appear at the school for my service in cleaning the classrooms and waiting on table for the student-boarders. There were less than twenty students then; the work was not heavy, but if I remember rightly, I received no payment. I do not remember now how long I stayed there, what knowledge I picked up in the classroom; one thing I remember is that I read Irving's *Sketch Book* there for the first time, in which the description of Westminster Abbey incited my sudden desire for England. The general influence of Stanford, silent, not unkind, courteous, encouraging, that I felt from the buildings, the surrounding view with trees, even the group of students, was, I confess, far deeper than my first impression of Harvard, or even Oxford of England; after all, the library and lectures are not the main things. As I said, I worked without payment at the Manzanita Hall; I began to feel uncomfortable in course of time, with my heelless shoes and dirty coat. I decided to work at the Menlo Park Hotel, Menlo Park, as a dish-washer, till I could put myself in a respectable shape.

The work was not light; I had to rise every morning before four o'clock, and my work was never finished till ten o'clock at night. It was about the time when Japan declared war with China; what a delight it was to read the paper with the battle news in my spare time! When the war was quite advanced, almost reaching the zenith of interest as Li Hang Chang, the appointed Chinese Special Envoy, had already left home for Bakan to meet Ito, my mind grew restless from a sudden burst of desire to see my friends at San Francisco, and talk over the war, if it were necessary, even to fight with them. I dismissed myself from the hotel, and hurried back again to the *San Francisco News*. I thought I was quite rich, as I had more than thirty dollars for my savings, while my companions at the office were in the same condition as before; I could not help feeling sorry for them, and then I bought a pair of shoes for A, a new shirt for B, and played a philanthropist for a short time. When I awoke from a few occasions of extravagance, I found myself again penniless as my friends. The paper needed somebody who could translate from the English papers; and I was asked to help it, even for a short time. As I had no particularly bright job before me, I consented to stay; under any circumstances, I thought I must put my fingers into their former order, as they had become swollen from the dirty dish-water with much soda. Even in America it is not easy to earn money.

Joaquin Miller was regarded most reverentially by Japanese as a *sennin*, or "hermit who lived on dews." His great personality, it was said, was in his denying of the modern civilisation; his only joy of life was to raise roses and carnations. I believe it was with more than curiosity that I climbed up the hills behind Oakland to see him at the "Heights," where he sang:

> *"Come under my oaks, oh, drowsy dusk!*
> *The wolf and the dog; dear incense hour,*
> *When Mother Earth hath a smell of musk,*
> *And things of the spirit assert their power—*
> *When candles are set to burn in the West—*
> *Set head and foot to the day at rest."*

It was the ideal spot on earth with balmy air, such a wonder of view at your feet; I fell in love with the place at once, and I thought I could get plenty of the rest which was beyond my reach during two years and seven months that I had already spent in America. More than the place itself, I fell in love with Mr. Miller, whose almost archaic simplicity in the way of living and speech was indeed prophet-like; he said he would be glad to have me stay with him. I decided to do so on the spot.

He said that he had no lesson or teaching to give me, or if he had any, it was about the full value of silence, without the understanding of which one could never read the true heart of Mother Nature; and the heart of Nature, he said, was Love.

"Silence, Love—and simplicity," he exclaimed.

When I retired in the house right next to his own to sleep that night, I secretly decided that I would become a poet.

II

I WAS HOEING ROUND AND watering the flowers in the plum orchard at the "Heights," when I received a letter from Gelett Burgess, then the editor of the *Lark*, the now famous, though short-lived, California magazine, saying: "I have several notices of your poems from the Eastern papers, and your work has been very well received." The July of 1896, when my five English poems (let me call them poems) were first printed by Mr. Burgess in the *Lark*, was certainly the dawn of my new page of American life; with his letter my heart jumped high in joy. Indeed, I confess that the joy I felt then was the greatest of joys, and I never felt anything like it again; to have it once in a lifetime may be said to be lucky enough. Before I sent my poems to the *Lark*, I submitted one poem to the editor of the *Chap Book*, Chicago, who wrote, when he printed it: "The current issue of the *Lark* contains some few pages of verses by Yone Noguchi, and I find that the pleasant opportunity I thought to have of first printing his writing is denied me. Perhaps I am a little envious." And the poem beginning, "Mystic spring of vapour," which was published in the *Philistine* in September, was bitterly attacked by a certain Mr. Hudson, of Oakland, as a plagiarism from Poe. I was a devout reader of Poe's poems; it was the only book, beside the work of our famous *kokku* poet, Basho Matsuo, and a book on Zen Buddhism by Kochi, that I brought to the "Heights." My name began to be known; newspaper men of San Francisco came up the hill to interview me. It was the *Examiner* that wished me to stand before a camera; alas, I had no decent white shirt to wear then. I borrowed one from my friend, which was two sizes too large; I found, when the picture was taken, that even my clenched fist might easily go in at the neck.

I published my own attitude toward Hudson's attack in the following fashion: "Let critics say what they please! Poetry is sacred to me. It is not *art* for me, but feeling. My poems are simply my own journal of feeling—the footmark of my experience. I can stand anything but deceiving myself. I am not sorry a bit, if there be an exact correspondence in shape. I am thankful to God for giving me the moment when I felt the same thing with Poe. I cannot understand why you could not feel the same thing with Poe if you want to. It is not poetry at all, if you must express yourself in some other fashion when you think of one thing."

When he again attacked me on "On the Heights" in the September *Lark*, he made himself a subject of laughter, even to the editor of the *Examiner*, who said: "The occurrence of the word 'window' in the first line of Noguchi's and the seventh line of the quoted section from Poe is, of course, a damaging affair for both, and when it is reinforced by the damning fact that 'beauty' is mentioned in the third verse of Noguchi and the fifth verse of the quotation from Poe, the candid reader must admit that the two writers spell according to the same dictionary. It is to be feared, however, that Poe's claims to originality are not on a much better foundation than those of Noguchi. Noah Webster had already published all the words of *The Sleeper* before Poe, and Dr. Johnson before Webster, and still others before Dr. Johnson."

Most of the Eastern literary magazines did not take Hudson's attack seriously; I was defended by many of them, the *Book Buyer*, for instance, who remarked: "He has originality enough, if that were the full equipment of a great writer. Beauty and delicacy of thought are in his work, and imagination to spare. But the imagery is often so exotic as to perplex, as when Oriental music falls on Western ears. But he did not steal his cadences from Poe, nor from anybody else."

I found in the various papers and weeklies poems or other writings addressed to me, mostly in kind and often humorous vein; let me quote one of them as a specimen:

YONE NOGUCHI
(To the tune of "He's No Farmer")

"Yone!—
As critics lift their carping bray,
Pretend thy hair is full of hay,
Mixed S. Crane middlings, longs and shorts,
With other Poe its odds and orts,
And ravelin shreds—they also say:
Homer is not awake alway,
Shakespeare caught flukes i' his bright sword-play.

Wordsworth is solemn at his sports,
(He is, Yone!)
But thou, train ever round thy lay
Some fragrant wilding of the May:
Graft not its stem with borrowed thoughts,
Nor trim the spray—it bloom aborts—
For public, Publishers PAY:
Then blossoms, clustering thick thy bay,
Shall crown thee, Yone!"

The death of the *Lark*, after a brilliant course of two years, was much lamented through the country; the *Chap Book* ended its note on the passing of the *Lark* with the following words: "And now it is dead. Les Jeunes, taken doubtless with an affection similar to the gold fever of the Klondyke, are striking out for the East, where the nuggets of recognition and encouragement are to be picked up in the fertile fields of literature and art. Gelett Burgess and Ernest Peixotto are in New York, Bruce Potter and Florence Lundborg are headed toward Europe, and 'the Homeless Snail,' Yone Noguchi, alone remains:

> 'Standing like a ghost in the smiling mysteries
> of the moon garden.'"

Indeed, I was left alone at Miller's "Heights" sadly or happily. It was happy to lie on the top of the hill when the poppies covered it in spring, where I often dreamed death would be, if I could be buried in such a place overlooking the bay (the Golden Gate), sweeter than life; it was happier still to rest by a brook in the canyon, with whose song I could send my mind far into the Unknown and Eternal. My life of seclusion was not without a happy break in meeting celebrities now and then.

My passion for wandering, that seemed to have ceased temporarily its flight (I was quite a traveller already in my boyhood at home), began to blaze up again; I felt it almost impossible not to heed the calling voice of trees, hills, waters, and skies in the far distance. I have read the romantic story of Goldsmith in his vagabondising in European villages, with only his beloved little flute; and the travelling note that was written by Basho, poet of moon and wind, impressed my mind, which only aspired to become a real poet. And the true poetry is not in writing, but in the union with nature. I decided to experience a "tramp life" in poetical fashion; I thought it was the first step for my idea. I did not see at all the hard side of it; the romantic aspect of parting with the world and society, the perfect freedom, the having all airs and flowers on equal terms, was brighter. It was the month of April when I started on my lone pilgrimage (with a book of poems instead of a holy staff) toward the Yosemite Valley; my tramp life commenced at Stockton, which I reached by a river boat from San Francisco. I remember clearly, as it were yesterday, that it was already dark, a few stars sparkling in the high sky, as if a guiding spirit for a pilgrim, when I passed through Chinese Camp, the once famous place I had read of in Harte's stories of a mining camp. I felt extremely sad, the wind blowing from behind, at not finding a right place to sleep, and finally I camped under the trees, by a brook whose silver song still remains in my ears. I could not fall asleep because my blanket was so light, and I remember I put many little stones and twigs on it, that I gathered under the starlight. It was the first time that I felt such a great love in that light, which I never felt before; I thank my tramp life, which revealed many new beauties of nature, above all, how to appreciate it. I wrote down my feeling of that night in *The Night Reverie in the Forest;* in one part I sang:

> *"O Repose, whose bosom harbours the heavenly dream-ships,*
> *welcome me, an exiled soul!*
> *Thou, Forest, where Peace and Liberty divide their*
> *wealth with even a homeless convict,*
> *Let me sleep in thine arm-boughs, safer far than a*
> *king's iron castle guarded by mortal power!"*

Then at the ending part:

> *"Ah Loneliness! Loneliness—to whom a boatman of*
> *God is the sole saviour on the vast Sea of Eternity!*
> *I repose under the forest's arm-bough—if I awaken not*
> *forever, pray, brother mortal,*
> *Make my grave under the greenest grass and carve*
> *these lines: 'Here sleeps a nameless Poet.'"*

I entered in the Courter Vale Road gradually, first coming into contact with California cedars, spruces, and pines. The season was still too early, as there were few travellers who had advanced into the valley; many houses by the road were still unoccupied, and consequently I could not find food and sleep at the place I wished. Once I slept in a barn, where I found no horse when I went to sleep. At midnight I felt a queer warmth and occasionally heard some biting sound, doubtless of hay; but I was too sleepy to rise. In the morning I found, to my surprise, I was sleeping right between the four legs of a horse. This and other incidents did not bring any pleasure at that time, like today, when I feel an almost tantalising delight in my reminiscent mood.

What a thrill of fear, which was not the thing of our world, I felt in the Yosemite Valley, as you can see in the first lines of my song of night:

> *"Hark! The prophecy-inciting windquake of the unfathomable*
> *concave of darkest Hell!*
> *O, the God-scorning demon's shout against the*
> *truth-locked gate of mighty Heaven!"*

What a sight of the falls reflected to the low-hanging moon! The tall trees looked no other but the ghosts or spirits who gathered and talked something wonderful and evil; and what a sound of water, besides that of the fall, which dashed down the river! I felt cold and suddenly hungry, when I became conscious of my sad being amid such an almost frightening demonstration of Nature, particularly in the night. I was kindly treated by the clerk or manager of the Stoneman House, who needed somebody to chop wood, as the hotel had opened only a week before; I was given good food that night, and I even slept in a bed. I stayed in the valley four days, during which I chopped wood, with one Indian boy, for whose brother I was taken by one person there; I took every chance to look around the valley as much as I could. When I left the hotel, the manager wished me to stay for the whole summer; but wages and work were not my aim. I left the valley light-hearted, as I entered. I took the train at Raymond on my way to San Francisco, as I had some money through the kindness of Mrs. S——, that dearest soul, to whom I dedicated my Yosemite book when it appeared.

My next, far longer tramp-journey in the month of April 1898, was toward the south, down to Los Angeles; as I had decided that I would chop wood for my dinner, and sleep in a barn, I had only a few dollars for an emergency, and a mishap that I encountered on the first night robbed them away. I was sleeping in an empty wagon car, which I found near the station of Ocean View; it was rather hot and uncomfortable; I was obliged to take off my trousers before lying down. But it was a mistake, as I found when, my car moving toward San Francisco at midnight, I hurriedly grasped my trousers upside down, and all the silver rolled away. I was glad, however, my little razor and comb were safe in the pocket of my coat; I was no more a boy, as a trifling moustache already began to bother me; and I had to have my toilet done before entering a town, by the looking-glass of a stream I might find. I wished to keep at least my appearance of a gentleman tramp.

I left San José in the early morning for Los Gatos, being given a chance to ride on a wagon by a kindly old farmer. As it was the latter part of April, both sides of the country road were perfectly covered by the cherry-blossoms in full glory. The morning freshness mingled with the fragrance of the flowers; as I was high up in the wagon, I was looking down the flat valley, and this unexpected flower-viewing (it is the Spring custom that Japanese keep at home) called my longing at once to sing my mind. The beauty of the cherry-blossom is not only Japan's; and it never happens in Japan to admire the thousand and thousand trees in one spot. I have the following in my diary of the journey:

"*Santa Cruz, April* 29*th*

Yesterday evening—a little before sunset—I crossed a long tunnel. Half a mile long, some say. The station-master did not believe me when I said that I was going to cross the tunnel. However, he assured me that there was some one hour before the next train. Enter did I. What dampness in the tunnel! It were the easiest thing to faint in it. A thievish light from the door, which was already small as a morning star, finally disappeared. Alas! Such darkness! I felt as if the darkness were an animal and about to devour my flesh. Monstrous darkness! I missed my footing and fell in the ditches. 'My God!' I exclaimed. I crawled, my hands touching the railroad track. Undoubtedly I might have been dead if I had not had Faith—Faith that would come out at the other side if I kept on. Oh, mighty Faith! Mother of hope! Yes, Faith is life! . . ."

It was fortunate, perhaps, to find a Japanese keeping a bamboo store or laundry shop, or working on a farm, wherever I went along the coast, who welcomed me, as my name was very well known to him; I was often begged to stay, if possible, indefinitely. I was glad that I could wash my stockings, or shirts even, with hot water prepared by him; he would be pleased also if I served him by writing an English letter or interpreting a business transaction. I stayed more than anywhere else at Monterey, where I learned the mystery of the sea better than ever; I inscribed my name in Japanese on the wall of the Carmel Mission, satisfied to find myself the only inscriber.

I reached San Lucas one afternoon of a certain day, feeling almost dead from hunger, as I had only breakfast on that day. The station-master directed me to a Japanese who kept a little vegetable garden; I found him quite ill, but his welcome was cordial. I saw plenty of charcoal fire burning to keep him warm; I think now that it was from the charcoal gas that I was suffocated and fell flat on the floor. It is true I was lying as a dead person till midnight, when the cold air brought me to my senses. I was told when I awoke that the sick man had had such a trouble in sending a message to San Francisco of my death, or at least of my being near to death. I understood the reason that I surprised my friends at Los Angeles with my presence a month later; I believe I was then supposed already dead throughout the Japanese colony of the coast. I thank the rain, the most gentle rain of Californian May, that drove me into a barn at San Miguel during two days, but made me study *Hamlet* line after line, which I carried with me; whatever I know about it today is from my reading in that haystack.

I cannot forget San Louis Obispo, where I entered under the bright moon, riding on the wagon of some gypsies with whom I became acquainted on the roadside; I parted from them presently with the hope of meeting again. I had not known before that it was a Spanish town full of beautiful girls; above all, with such a sweet atmosphere which only belongs to a Latin race; I observed that many of the girls were sitting with their banjos by the balconies, and singing serenades. When I appealed to them at one house with my hunger and tired feet, they stopped their songs, and rushed into a kitchen to cook something for me; I believe that it was a sort of festival in the town, as the joyous uproar could not be mistaken. How those young girls with such large black eyes and olive-skinned oval faces, sympathised with me when I told them I had walked so many miles on that day! Nothing particular happened before I reached Los Angeles in the beginning of July, except my stay of one month at Santa Barbara, where I was picked up as a dishwasher by some Eastern visitor, who had settled there temporarily for health. I remember only one thing, that I made the young lady of the house angry, who was evidently a lover of poetry, particularly of Longfellow, as it seemed, by saying that he was only a poet for such a stupid head like hers.

I was already in Chicago in 1900, writing my own impression of that city for the *Evening Post* there; and then my head further turned eastward, to New York, and London across the ocean.

III

Joaquin Miller

I

I MUST GO BACK TO my nineteenth year to write on Joaquin Miller from the beginning. I heard his name first, I distinctly remember, from my fellow-countryman, then a student at Stanford, who dropped into the dirty kitchen of Menlo Park Hotel (where I was temporarily employed as a dish-washer) to cheer me up and also to have a secret bit of pie. The poet's life amid the roses, quite high above the cities and people (my friend told me as best he could what he knew about him), made me sadder when I compared it with my life, in which my fingers grew all swollen, disfigured from using soda in the dish-water; and it was about the time that I began to read English poetry. But Joaquin Miller was dismissed from my mind till five or six months later, when I found myself again in San Francisco and cast my lot with the office of the *Soko Shimbun,* a Japanese newspaper, for the second time; when I one day found Miller's name in Webster's Dictionary, my reverence toward him doubled at once. I do not remember now to whom it was that I told of my great despair of American life; surely it was he that suggested to me the home of Joaquin Miller, the "Heights" he called the place, at the back hill of Oakland, when I wished to find some place to sleep and read without doing much manual work. I was told by him to be sure of Miller's great love of Japan and the Japanese, and above all, of his eccentric way of living; and he said further, I believe, that he would doubtless gladly let me live with him since some young Japanese had already such an experience before. When I decided to make my call on him, I took all the books that I had, six or seven, excepting a copy of Poe's poems as I was already his admirer, to a certain second-hand bookshop to raise my travelling expense.

The scene of my first meeting with Miller floats most clearly, most sweetly before my eyes as if it were only yesterday, although it is now a matter of almost twenty years ago. I know how I trembled when I stepped on the somehow unsafe narrow wooden path or bridge at the entrance, leading me directly to his ridiculously small cottage; I believe

I should have run away from the sudden failing of my courage (as I said before I was not yet then fully nineteen) if a young girl, a Mexican or half Negress, Miss Alice as I found afterward (we were good friends during my stay at the "Heights"), who had just stepped out of the cottage, had not encouraged me with her friendly smile. Joaquin Miller, who at once reminded me of my imaginary picture of childhood days for a certain *Tengu* or Mountain Elf with red long nose, whose supernatural power made Yoshitsune Minamoto a great swordsman in Japanese legend, stretched out his hand from the bed (he lived practically in a cottage of one room) when he saw me entering. I thought how romantically impressive he looked. It was his habit, as I soon found out, to "loaf and invite his own soul" lying in bed the whole forenoon; a silken skullcap which he wore gave him the most interesting touch of an older age. When I told him of my desire in climbing up the hill, he exclaimed "Welcome! Welcome!" Then he wished me to accompany him to his old mother's to dine together, when Miss Alice (a sweet soul who, it is said, died some years ago somewhere in Southern America) came and announced dinner. On our way to Mrs. Miller's cottage, which stood some one hundred yards up the hill, Joaquin Miller picked abundantly the roses white or red, which he scattered over the large dinner table, exclaiming: "God bless you!" I must not forget to tell you that he wore top-boots and, wonder of all, a bearskin over his shoulders even while eating; a red crêpe sash was tied round his waist most carelessly. His dress was of corduroy. But I noticed that there was a large diamond ring on a finger of his right hand which threw an almost menacing brilliancy. He was six feet tall; his white beard fully covered his breast. Had I ever seen before, I asked myself, any more striking person than this Miller, the Poet of the Sierras? Indeed I accepted him without any question for the very symbol of romance and poetry of which my young mind often dreamed; I congratulated myself that the most happy accident had brought me to the right spot where my real soul would surely grow. What pleased me best, I confess, was Miller's manner in calling me "Mr. Noguchi," as it was the first occasion to hear myself so addressed since my arrival in California; hitherto I had been a Charley or a Frank according to the employer's fancy. When this unexpected joy of mine grew deeper and I became, in spite of myself, suddenly silent and solemn, the old lady, now dead for many years (Miller once play-fully exclaimed, when I remarked that a Japanese sparrow in our proverb did not forget to dance even in its hundredth year: "Why, my mother is that Japanese bird!") slyly looked upon me from the other side of the table and even winked; now that wink of hers might have been her apology for her son's eccentricity, mistaking my silence for accusation. Never did I think Miller was particularly eccentric, never even once during my long stay with him; he was the most natural man; and his picturesqueness certainly was not a crime. When Mrs. Miller began to say something, the poet exclaimed offhand that eating was a sacred service; and said, "Mother, you talk too much; mother, mother, you keep quiet. Silence! Again silence! Silence helps your digestion. Eat slowly, all of you, think of something higher, and be content!" The dinner was the simplest ever I ate in an American household, but the most satisfactory.

That evening I descended the hill again for the newspaper office at San Francisco, where I had to bid my goodbye to my friends; and I thought that I would buy a pair of top-boots if I could raise money enough somewhere, even though the bearskin were out of reach. When I left the city for the "Heights" the next day, I carried with me the *Hokku* poems by Basho Matsuo and a book of the Zen philosophy of Kochi Zenji, besides my beloved Poe's poems; it was already evening when I reached Miller's after leaving the Fruitvale car at Dimond as I had before, with the lightest heart like that of a breeze or bird. I found Miller hoeing round the garden and watering the roses. He was singing something; when I asked him what he sang, he said it was Omar's following verse:

> "Each Morn a thousand Roses brings, you say;
> Yes, but where leaves the Rose of Yesterday?"

It was the first time I heard the name of Omar, on whom, one year later, Mr. Garnet wrote a song for the *Lark*, a little California magazine, and dedicated it to me. I confess that I soon began to assume the rustic rôle of that Persian poet.

Oh that unforgettable first night at the "Heights," when I slept indeed far nearer to the stars; yes, I slept perfectly surrounded by those steadfast stars of whom Keats was thinking on his deathbed. There were the stars everywhere, the stars in the skies and the stars on the earth; who could tell, I thought, where the lights left off and the stars began? Really a thousand lights of some ten villages below under our feet magically turned to stars in night's misty air. I was glad that my eyes suddenly began to open to what was good and beautiful in Nature. And what a dawn and sunrise I observed next morning! It is not too much to say that one lived partly in the clouds at this place; the mists, rolling above the towns, will soon lift, rifting little by little, and presently many a church spire will be pointing up; and pray, look down over the San Francisco Bay, nay, the mobile floor of dustless silver! And another wonder shall be waiting for you at evening. I raised my head and looked down through the western window of my little cottage attached to Miller's; where my eyesight reached far away was the gate of the Bay, and lo! there the golden sun was sinking heavily down through that gate, as if a mighty king or poet at his departure for "Far Beyond." When I was told afterward by Miller that this was the very place where John C. Freemont, the path-finder, once pitched his tent and was inspired to give the name of Chrysopylae or Golden Gate, the place became thrice more romantic.

I was pleased it was the month of May with the deepening shadows of the acacia trees; one large bamboo chair under the tree by the narrow entrance bridge, at the front of the cottage or cottages, delighted me, as I thought I could freely play there a Hindoo monk in meditation, perhaps the Dharuma who, it is said, sat still during nine long years before he arose with his new religion, on whom I wrote:

> *"Let us return to the elements and dusts,*
> *Let us in dust find our own salvation!*
> *O bit of dust, Dharuma, O body of light!"*

How I thought Miller was unpoetical, even despised his cruelty when one or two years later he cut down that large acacia tree. What music of the birds at the "Heights" in May! How delighted I was with the simple song of the meadow lark, even when it could not aspire like Shelley's skylark. You will see here butterflies passing by the cottage in tremendous haste, some dropping in to rest on the table for awhile; and you will be frightened by the sudden sight of a squirrel popping out from the most unexpected corner in the purple spring air. When the months advanced toward the summer, the hills were covered by the flowers singing and laughing, their treasures spilled far up and far down everywhere. One morning Miller brought to me a bunch of poppies ("The golden poppy is God's gold" is Miller's song), saying that they were the State flower by act of the Legislature; I exclaimed: "Such a tiny flower for such a big State!" Miller said then: "The sweetest flowers grow closest to the ground; you must not measure Nature by its size: if there is any measure, it will be that of beauty; and where is beauty there is truth. First of all, you must know Nature by yourself, not through the book. It would be ten thousand times better to know by your own knowledge the colour, the perfume and the beauty of a single tiny creeping vine in the valley than to know all the Rocky Mountains through a book; books are nothing. Read the history written on the brows of stars!"

I confess that it was my disappointment, however, not to find books at Miller's place; not only in my cottage but also in Miller's sanctum or Holy Grotto, as I used to call it, I hardly saw anything that might pass for a book. When I found a book or books in my cottage, they were nailed high up near the ceiling; it might have been perhaps Miller's idea to make them stand for decoration. Although he lighted neither lamp nor candle at night ("My life is like the life of a bird," Miller often declared), and professed he would awaken when the sun rose, I could not conform myself with his rule; I got a few candles to read the books which I brought down from the walls. They were all Miller's old books; it was in this way that I made my first acquaintance with his early poems or what-not. But what interested me most was a little book of his reminiscences in which I read how he appeared in London with his poems, how he failed with many other English publishers and finally with Murray, whom he had kept for the last (because he felt sure that Byron's publisher would be his); in this bit of autobiography he writes:

"The great Murray took me upstairs when I told him I had a book all about the great West of America, and there he showed me many pictures of Byron—Byron's mother among the rest—a stout, red-faced woman with awful fat arms and low black curls about a low narrow brow.

"I ventured to say she looked good-natured.

"'Aye, now, don't you know she would shy a poker at your head, don't you know?' And the great Murray wagged his finger in her face as he said this, quite ignoring me, my presence or my opinion. Then he spun about on his heel to where I stood in the background, and, taking sight at me behind his long, lean finger, jerked out the words: 'Now, young man, let us see what you have got.'

"I drew forth my first born of London town and laid it timidly in his hand. He held his head to one side, flipped the leaves, looked in, jerked his head back, looked in again, twisted his head like a giraffe, and then lifted his long finger.

"'Aye, now, don't you know poetry won't do? Poetry won't do, don't you know?'

"'But will you not read it, please?'

"'No, no, no. No use, no use, don't you know.'

"I reached out my hand, took the despised sheets, and in a moment was in the street, shaking my fist at that house now and then as I stopped in my flight and turned to look back with a sort of nervous fear that he had followed me."

But when he published soon afterward his first London book at his own expense, the success was most instant; and all the praise upon those *Songs of the Sierras* in the pages of the *Athenæum*, the *Academy*, the *Saturday Review*, the *Westminster Review*, and many others were quite uniform. The following, it is said, was what the *Spectator* selected to show the real presence of no common power in Miller:

> "I lay in my hammock: the air was heavy
> And hot and threatening; the very heaven
> Was holding its breath, and bees in a bevy
> Hid under my thatch; and birds were driven
> In clouds to the rocks in a hurried whirr
> As I peered down the path for her;
> She stood like a bronze bent over the river,
> The proud eyes fixed, the passion unspoken,
> When the heavens broke like a great dyke broken.
> Then ere I had fairly time to give her
> A shout of warning, a rushing of wind,
> And the rolling of clouds and a deafening din,
> And a darkness that had been black to the blind,
> Came down as I shouted, 'Come in! Come in!
> Come under the roof, come up from the river,
> As up from the grave—come now or come never!'
> The tasselled tops of the pines were as weeds,
> The torn woods rocked like to lakeside reeds,
> And the world seemed darkened and drowned forever."

And I had once an occasion, when I lived with him, to read a copy of Froude's letter to Alfred Graves concerning Miller's book, which I found under the dusts of old papers in his cottage; the historian wrote:

"I opened it, expecting nothing, and was at once struck with its unusual character. Instead of speculative maunderings or unsolvable problems or vague aspirations after a state of things which if realised would induce me for one to blow my brains out, so destitute the earth would appear, I find the ring of genius, human life and human passion of which the very sounds had almost been forgotten."

Then he added: "Do not compare him to Walt Whitman. You might as well compare a young half-broken Arab to a circus piebald broken loose from the troupe and gone mad." (It is rather amusing to think whether Froude, if he were living today, would say the same thing.)

II

ALTHOUGH I GENERALLY AGREE WITH the *Times* critic's comparison of Joaquin Miller with Gordon of Australia ("These two poets were set on horseback, and they rode up the slopes of Parnassus until the loftier steeps cast them back," is the ending phrase of his recent interesting article on Miller), this American poet I used to know in 1895–9 was not a melodramatic centaur on swift galloping hooves in song, but the singer of "a brother soul in some sweet bird, a sister spirit in a rose," not the maker of loud-voiced ballads like the tide of a prairie fire or the marches of the Sierra mountains, but the dove-meek poet of love and humanity which, in Miller's words, grow best and sweetest in silence. It is singular enough that he could not forget, even when he sang on silence as in the following, his former love of exuberance, colour, and concert rhythm:

> *"Aye, Silence seems some maid at prayer,*
> *God's arm about her when she prays*
> *And where she prays and everywhere,*
> *Or storm-strewn days or sundown days—*
> *What ill to Silence can befall*
> *Since Silence knows no ill at all?*
>
> *Vast Silence seems some twilight sky*
> *That leans as with her weight of stars*
> *To rest, to rest, no more to roam,*
> *But rest and rest eternally.*
> *She loosens and lets down the bars,*

> *She brings the kind-eyed cattle home,*
> *She breathes the fragrant field of hay*
> *And heaven is not far away."*

I soon found out, when I made my own home with him, that my Japanese temperament and thought should be kept far apart from his own, and I must live and grow independently like a lone star in solitude; to make a Miller out of myself, I thought at once would be absurd and foolish. When he declared on my very first day at the "Heights" that he had nothing to teach me, I took such a language itself for a great teaching and reverence to another's individuality; and when he proposed that we should live in different cottages communicating as little as possible, I thought that he too, like a Japanese Buddha monk, a student of Silence's sigh and mystery, knelt before the sad shrine of Solitude with the fire of faith burning within. I admired him when he stood, to use the phrase of my poem, as one scorning the swords and wanton menace of cities (how he hated to appear in town!); and he was so pleased to see me, again to use the phrase of my poem, a victor of Life and Silence upon the "Heights." As I said before, I spent with him four long years; but how little we spoke to each other during those years. Even when we went together to the cañon to cut trees or build a bridge, or hunt a quail for Mrs. Miller's breakfast (we often returned carrying only one or two English sparrows), or when we went together to plant a tree under mists or rain at the back hill, or picked together the plums (Miller had a plum orchard), or watered together the garden roses, I strictly observed his rule of "No debating of any sort;" but when his spirit moved to talking on Nature, he talked on her economy, and said: "Nature wastes nothing—nothing; least of all does Nature waste time. And she is never in haste. Remember to go slowly and diligently toward the stars. Silence! And no debating there! What a saving of time!"

I never asked him, not even once, what was his art of poetry, or what methods he had; it would be certainly futile to think you might study or even mention poetry when you lived here at the "Heights," where, as I wrote once:

> *"My feeling was that I stood as one*
> *Serenely poised for flight, as a muse*
> *Of golden melody and lofty grace."*

Suppose you lay down, with your face toward the Bay of the Golden Gate, upon the highest spot of the "Heights" covered by the poppies and buttercups in May, perhaps near the large stone monument under which Miller is now sleeping (I bought the white paint, when the monument was finished in 1897, and inscribed by Miller's order the words, "To the Unknown" on a little stone by its side); when Keats' last words, that he already seemed to feel the flowers growing over himself, come to your mind, I believe that you would be glad to be kissed by Death and say: "I see already the butterflies beaming over my head." Suppose again the mists (how Miller hated to use the word "fogs") marching from the oceans like the ghost-battalions, took possession of the "Heights" some winter morning; it would be the day when my Japanese mind always entered into our mythology, and I even felt as if I were the first god, Izanami, standing on the "Floating Bridge of Heaven," before the creation. Again on such a morning I used to hear Miller's recitation of *Columbus*, his best poem by general consent, in which his voice, as the word of the Admiral in that poem, leapt like a leaping sword:

"Sail on! Sail on! Sail on! And on!"

Oh sail on? And where? Why, we had only to sail on to the home of poesy.

To live in poetry is ten times nobler than merely to write it; to understand it well is certainly far more divine than to speak it on the tongue. If there ever was a poet who fully lived or practised poetry, it was that Joaquin Miller, even though he may not have been a great poet of words (and I am no fit person to speak on his written poems as I am so different from him); and he sufficiently proved the fact of his living in poetry at the "Heights" as God's gardener as he pleased to call himself. It was his hope to build a City Beautiful; he failed, doubtless, if that City meant the communion or fellowship of men. But I think that he tried his best in the building and was even successful as far as his part only was concerned.

Once we talked on Japan and things Japanese; our talk came to the subject of the cherry-tree. He said:

"Don't you know that the Lord God planted a garden eastward in Eden wherein He caused to grow everything that is pleasant to the sight and good for food? Observe that the tree pleasant to the sight comes first! Indeed it comes first! And the trees good for food are considered last. It is happy to know that of all the thousand of famous Japanese cherry-trees there is not one that bears a cherry that even a bird would eat. The Japanese cherry-trees are all and only pleasant to the sight. That is really fine."

And such is the keynote of his way of living and also of the building of the City Beautiful; his thirty years' patience and earning were gladly given to the "Heights," whose original state, I am sure, would have been a forgotten bit of waste.

When Miller entrusted me to arrange his old writings printed in papers and magazines which he happened to preserve, I used my wisdom to copy out the best and striking passages in a little book, in which today I find the following:

"I was once riding alone over the mountains of Durango, in Northern Mexico, when I was overtaken by what I thought to be a band of robbers. There was no escaping them—there was but one mountain road climbing up the back of the great, steep, rugged mountain; and so I did the best I could—joined them and fell into conversation with the leader, half expecting all the time to be murdered.

"At last, as we climbed the lofty summit and looked down over the rich valley, with its cool waters winding through it, this black, hard-looking Mexican reined his mule, lifted his hat, and, looking over the valley, exclaimed: 'Que Hermosa!' 'How beautiful!' I felt no fear after that. We slept together that night; and he told me, this man who could not read, many pretty things for my books."

Miller often remarked that one who had eyes to see beauty was always truthful; where he said truth he justly meant beauty; and again when he said beauty, it would not be much wrong to say that he meant plain common sense. He declared: "Why, the true poetry is nothing but the common sense. Truth, beauty and again truth—the right heart! No poet can create or destroy one particle of truth or beauty or common sense, any more than he can create or destroy a particle of gold. He can only give it a new form, garment it with splendour, and set it in a new light. Were I to try to define poetry, I should say that poetry is the divinely beautiful woman truth (that is beauty and plain common sense in Miller's understanding), gorgeously, yet modestly and most perfectly gowned. Therefore where there is poetry, there is light, again there is joy."

I decided from the beginning when I first climbed the hill, to pay him with my service, to speak plainly, for my board and room at the

"Heights;" so I was pleased to make coffee in the morning and cook his dinner when he was not dining with his mother. To cook outside, when the weather was fine with the so-called Italian sky, over the camp fire, by a little brook which always reminded me of Tennyson's poem, was a perfect delight. It was while I was blowing the fire or peeling the potatoes or onions that I was often frightened by unexpected thoughts and fancies. The cooking was simple; I had to boil a lump of beef, that is when we had it, in a large iron pot for two hours by Miller's direction. He never said a word even when I cooked badly, provided I allowed him to season the broth; he always remarked that Longfellow, Lowell, and all the others loved high seasoning as he. It was Miller's work, when we had to dine on the table under the rose bushes, to place a linen cloth over it; he would pick up a few little stones to weigh down the cloth, when winds might blow. When he brought out his claret bottle, it was the time when he wished to stay by the table for two or three hours, our usual dinner time at the "Heights" or this Garden of Eternity.

My Japanese mind was glad that Miller was kind to his mother; he served her reverently, saying, "Mother is first." Such a devotion, I thought, had a firm foundation not so much in the blood impulse as in his recognition of Life's hardest battle which this staunch German woman ever fought (what a suffering, what patience she must have undergone since the day when she took her family to Oregon from Indiana in Miller's thirteenth year); she was the soul who inspired him with the song called the *Bravest Battle*, in which he sang:

> *"Yet, faithful still as a bridge of stars,*
> *She fights in her walled-up town—*
> *Fights on and on in the endless wars,*
> *Then silent, unseen—goes down."*

I remember that more than once I was asked by Miller, when he returned home with many pieces of gold coin from San Francisco where he sold his writings, to take some of those glittering things to Mrs. Miller even at night; that was partly, I believe, from a desire to prove to her that he too could make money when he wished. Miller brought back a few small real nuggets chained to his watch from the Klondyke; it was his first act to present one of them to his mother.

Those four years I spent at the "Heights" were the hardest of my American life, as I often depended on the generosity of my Japanese friends even for my car fares. Since I had no money when I had to appear in San Francisco, I was frequently obliged to walk five or six miles to Oakland where one of my friends was washing dishes in a certain family. I could not pay to have my hair cut, so I let it grow freely; the people did not know the real condition when they laughed, saying that I was assuming a Milleresque affectation or pose. Once Miller called on me at a dirty Japanese boarding-house of San Francisco where I was temporarily staying for my purpose to read the books at the city library (there I read Francis Thompson for the first time); when he saw that I was washing my worn-out cotton stockings, he went out and bought me two pairs of decent woollen things. That was the only occasion I received anything from Miller; not one cent passed between us during the long four years. I began to write poems from my second year at the "Heights;" Miller's cañon (by the way his ground covered, it was said, some seventy acres), where Bryant's *Thanatopsis* always came to my mind, was my favourite retreat; from my mad desire to lay my soul to the heart of Nature as nakedly as possible, I carried my blankets under the trees of the cañon and slept there night after night in the month of July. It was in those nights that Miller often made his presence at the place to make himself assured of my safety, and brought for me at such an occasion something to eat as I might have been hungry. He watched carefully, but after his own fashion, over my welfare, as once a San Francisco paper remarked, as if a mother lion after a baby lion.

The "Heights" was God's property (using Miller's words), so that any picnic party had all the freedom of the place; it was our custom, when they had gone, to go round and pick up all the paper napkins and dirty baskets which they left behind. The friend-visitors were not few; Miller was often obliged to shut his door lest his peace and thought be disturbed; but the people who were so fortunate to strike the hours of his leisure and good humour into the bargain, would have the pleasure of hearing his Indian song, which was the prayer for rain, and it was my work, when the song began, to turn the pipe hidden under the roof of my cottage to make the water fall from above, and make Miller exclaim that his prayer was answered. Saturday was his market day, when he went down the hill to San Francisco or Oakland to buy one week's provisions; while he was away, I used to clean his cottage or sanctum. I wrote down this our pastoral lives at the "Heights" in the *American Diary of a Japanese Girl*, I as Miss Morning Glory, and Miller as the Poet Heine. I have the following on a certain day of that playful book:

"I volunteered to clean his holy grotto.

"The little cottage brought me a thought of one Jap sage who lived by choice in a ten-foot-square mountain hut. The venerable Mr. Chomei Kamo wrote his immortal *Ten-foot-square Record*. A bureau, a bed, and one easy-chair—everything in the poet's abode inspires repose—occupy every bit of space in Mr. Heine's cottage. The wooden roof is sound enough against a storm. A fountain is close by his door. Whenever you desire you may turn the screw and hear the soft melody of rain."

"That's plenty. What else do you covet?

"The closetlessness of his cottage is a symbol of his secretlessness. How enviable is an open-hearted gentleman! Women can never tarry even a day in a house without a closet. He never closes his door through the year.

"A piece of wire is added to his entrance at night. He would say that would keep out the tread of a dog and a newspaper reporter.

"Oh such a dust!

"I swept it.

"But I thought philosophically afterward, why should people be so fussy with the dust, when things are but another form of dust? What a far-away smell the dust had! What an ancient colour!"

III

I saw him for the last time at the "Heights" in 1904 on my way home from New York; as it was still in the time of the Russia-Japan War, we had much talk over the affair; he was so enthusiastic with Japan's victory. And he read to me many poems on Japan he had written; he was pleased when I suggested to him a book of collaboration under the title of *Japan of Sword and Love*. On its appearance in Tokyo (1905) a critic of the *Chronicle*, Kobe, used his bitter words of accusation, not on the poems but on Miller's article, the *Little Brown Men of Nippon*, which formed a sort of appendix; it is not worth while to dwell on Miller's absurdity, for which the critic had his own basis, but he finished up the review with the following words:

"But our readers have probably had enough by this time of Mr. Joaquin Miller, and will begin to have serious doubts of his sanity. His statements are not worth serious consideration, and they would not receive notice from us were it not that Mr. Yone Noguchi, himself a Japanese, prints such an effusion and lets its absurdities go forth to the world without question. He must be perfectly well aware that there is scarcely a sentence in the article which Mr. Miller has written which is not false either in actual statement or in implication, and yet he permits it to appear in a book published by himself as if Mr. Miller's phrensy were a sober statement of facts relating to Japan. Is it claimed that Joaquin Miller may properly play fast and loose with truth because he is classed as a poet?"

Then I duly wrote a letter to the editor of the paper; in part I said:

"It is one of the dangers they voluntarily meet, that they set their critical eyes only on the details and perfectly forget to see what Truth is hidden behind. I used to be delighted with the late Whistler's *à la Japonaise* pictures, which were merely a confusion of absurdities as Japanese pictures, but revealed his interesting personality and at the same time his own point of view. And Mr. Miller always exaggerates things. But his exaggeration is poetical. Only he puts his own thoughts in the most interesting way. And his telling things is always interesting, however groundless. And his personality which runs through his writing seems to me quite remarkable. I value his point of view. He may mislead the superficial readers involuntarily, but the profound people who do enjoy thoughts more than facts will be given some good points."

Suppose, what then, if the following, for instance, is a groundless even false statement:

"On almost every corner of the great thoroughfare is set a great earthern jar with dippers, ice and tea. Here old and young, mostly the children to and from school, help themselves. I know nothing more beautiful than a group of these little flower-pots tipping up to the big decorated and highly coloured jar of iced tea to help one another, the biggest little boy, cap in one hand and dipper in the other, helping the lesser ones. He gives twice to each one. And if a little sister in sandals and flower-like silk wrapper is of the party, he gives her an extra bow and a smile that is as beautiful as it is sincere. The city appoints the place for these tea-jars, but they are kept replenished by venerable parties, mostly kindly old women, who remain entirely unknown save to the authorities."

I am glad that we published that little book of poems together, since it contains Miller's *At Vespers in Tokyo* with the following poetical lines somewhere:

> *"Of all fair lands to look upon,*
> *To feel, to breathe, at Orient dawn,*
> *I count this baby land the best,*
> *Because here all things rest and rest*

And all men love all things most fair
And beautiful and rich and rare;
And women are as cherry-trees
With treasures laden, brown with bees.

Of all loved lands to look upon
Give me this loved land of Nippon,
Its bright, brave men, its maid at prayer,
Its peace, its carelessness of care.
A mobile sea of silver mist
Sweeps up for morn to mount upon;
Then yellow, saffron, amethyst—
Such changeful hues has blessed Nippon!
See but this sunrise then forget
All scenes, all suns, all lands save one
Just matin sun and vesper sun;
This land of inland seas of light;
This land that hardly recks of night."

Certainly they have an equally weird swing of charm that we find in Whistler's *à la Japonaise* pictures.

He was an idealist and a dreamer after his own picturesque way; since the literature of today, as some one pleases to remark, is perhaps the literature of Shaw and Masefield, Joaquin Miller belongs to the former age, when the quest of reality was not so important.

IV

Chicago (1900)

I

Now, after such an incessant ride of three days and nights from a boy town on the Pacific coast, I am here for a little time to study the great Chicago.

Chicago! What do I feel, do you ask? I feel really, as if I was taken by a devil to the City of Men, far beyond reach of mountain or river. It acted on me as a great dream of surprise; that tremendous railroad train took my breath away completely. Do you know I am a shy, without-knowledge-of-the-world poet—a little useless poet one hundred years late, using myself to dream in solitude! I kept me quiet as a star of spring night, I was breathing in indolence.

Now, when the devil, the great overland train, fled with me over 2000 miles during only a few days—how in the world can I be without excitement, without losing myself?

Please let me find repose and some fresh water. Is it impossible to secure me a pure water as in California? A thick sediment of mud or sand at the bottom of the glass is no harm, you say? Chicago water is horrible.

Did I recover my breath and set my ideas in correct order; what should I say first on Chicago?

Look! The Chicagoans are all alive; indeed, they are rushing on like a storm; they are jumping in clanging street cars. I saw here for the first time in my life such a dangerous procession of street cars—cars above my head, cars under my feet, cars everywhere, in this great city. Yes, sir, no one is sleeping in Chicago; no one is dying in Chicago. Chicago is the wonder, the City of Men; not a city of women, not a city of nature, of course.

Do you ask me if men interest me more than birds or trees? You want me to say that what interests me most is human nature, don't you? Yes, I find new interest in people since I came to the City of Men—Chicago.

Hello, my dear San Francisco; I am a Chicago boy now! Good-bye, my friends on the Pacific coast! Pray, let me be bold enough to speak truth: California—thank God I could get out of California— San Francisco, to speak more accurately, is simply an insane asylum. Chicago is a crazy city also as I see.

Chicago women—I speak of course only of the thousands of unfortunate whom need or madness keeps daily in the streets and offices downtown. These, I observe curiously, have, it would appear, no perfect balance. How is it possible to grow wise, or gentle, or serene, when they are talking loud all day, raising their voices in competition with the roar of the city's thousand strident voices? If two are together, always they are talking—never silent. They make such a mad noise in meeting as do morning sparrows hunting a breakfast. They do not know that peace and quiet are verily necessary to make anything grow; flowers do not grow well in the noiseful city, but they need the peace of the country; the flowers themselves keeping silence, of course, and it is exactly the same with human beings. They might say, however, that they are making practice to go to the platform of woman suffrage.

I said that San Francisco is simply an insane asylum. Worse than that, her people have made a science of robbery; they would even "steal the eyes out of a running horse." They are misunderstanding the meaning of "go-aheadism," which is the true American pride, as they are misunderstanding the true character of liberty. They are amuck with the weapons of power. It is a dangerous business to hand a butcher's knife to a maniac.

San Francisco gave me, doubtless, some happy hours. She kept me many a year with three things. What a glory! What a grandeur! You stand facing the Pacific Ocean at the Cliff House, and listen to the mighty songs of the greatest organist, the youngest and oldest minstrel for man and truth! That ocean's deepest shadowy songs are eternal inspiration, heavenly messages, the outpouring of the power of God. What a pity— how useless the ocean singing day and night such grand songs to the vulgar American, you might think! The vulgar American is the worst person in the world, being deaf and blind to nature. How long would the ocean, you might wonder, sing for a man who was dead a long time ago?

How long would the ocean continue to sing for Truth that had departed from the world? What a shame to have the divine ocean facing the nasty advertisement of "The Girl from Paris," or of some one's beer! It is a disgrace, San Franciscans, which you must correct. The tasteless advertisements merely spoil the beauty of the natural scenery. The Japanese Government gave a wise judgment when it forbade to post advertisements at the beautiful Higashi Yama, Kyoto, in the time the National Exposition was held.

The Americans carry their business atmosphere wherever they go; in their footsteps always they leave behind the unagreeable smell of commerce; they are like one who scatters around some ill odour.

I myself, however, have had many a glorious hour with the ocean, laying me on the graceful shore: what a joy it was to fall in sleep hearing the simple, great, honest masculine lullaby of that ocean!

The San Francisco girls sting you often as a wasp; they have the grace and small waist of the wasp. Their golden hair is dyed in the everlasting sunshine and the freshest air; their eyes are fallen stars of dreamy summer night; their footsteps are light and soft as the fluttering wing of the morning butterfly; they are so glad to show their well-shaped shoes and slender ankles by raising daintily their skirts. How happy I felt mingling among them! I was perfectly intoxicated with their beautiful faces as with wine. Their sharp, melodious voice was a queen's command to me.

I became tired with them all; I needed change. I left the Pacific coast.

But how long can I stand with this Chicago? Only God knows.

I tell you, oh how sad I felt not seeing any star at the night of my arrival! Stars are not kind to Chicago.

If the most noisy place is hell—surely Chicago must be hell. The only quiet thing I have seen in Chicago is the water of the Lake of Michigan.

Chicago is the city of cars and wagons. Chicago is the city of high buildings—did I expect to see a twenty-story-high-building in my life, I who being a Japanese used to living in a ridiculously small house, like a bird's home? Chicago is the city of dusts, smoke and littered streets. Certainly there are plenty of chances for negroes to make fortunes polishing shoes and dusting coats.

Chicago is the city of dirty creatures; there are many ragged, barefooted boys in and out and through the crowded lanes of trade, the human street-sparrows. Chicago is the city of pig killing and pork packing—the Chicagoans ought to be fat with the native production, the greasy pork, but on the contrary they are rather thin but firm in construction. They are not so handsome as the Californians; their complexion is not fair, their hands and feet are large.

One thing, however, that strikes me most forcibly in walking on the streets of Chicago is the total absence of stupid-looking faces—there is not even one sleepy mortal, I tell you. How foolishly the Japanese look in brown skin and dreamy eyes! Brown itself is the colour of melancholy and stupidity; but it shows some sweetness and pleads guilty to contentment. Brown is like night. The white-skinned Americans are like the day; they are the people of hard working, as the daytime is the time of work. The Orientals are the people of rest and dreams.

The Americans—that means the Chicagoans, since Chicago is the typical city of this great republic of riches and business—are nothing if they do not work hard, as the clock is nothing if it do not move. The Chicagoans were born to work hard; even beggars—lazy enough to beg—in Chicago handle a music machine.

Oh, what a feverish activity! The Chicagoans are never still, never pause to think; they are not at rest. Even when they are sitting they must be on the move; they talk loud on modern topics—on flying machines or the elopement of a society belle. Look at the rocking-chair habit of Americans—a part of their scheme of perpetual motion, nowhere else so nearly achieved!

Why do the Chicagoans work so hard? For happiness? I hardly believe they are working for happiness, but I believe they are working because they love work; they simply like to go ahead; they cannot be lazy; they are the overland train.

Americans, if I mistake them not, are not a people with serious ambitions. Chicago, the typical American city, is the representative of "go-aheadism." And Chicago has not much brain, but has the most wonderful physical power.

II

LET ME SEE YOUR FACE a moment, my dear Chicago—don't be scared, I shall not hurt you! Well, well—say, did you wash your face this morning, or do you wash every day? I suppose you never wash the face. How can you be looking so smoky if you wash?

O Lord, what is that overflowing in the sky—that vast, writhing flood of blackness? A Chicagoan said: "That's merely a smoke." "Merely a smoke," you say? Merely a smoke that divorces the sun and his bride the flower; that shuts out heaven from the sight of men? Now I see that the Chicagoans cannot be either clean-faced or clear-souled under such a terrible darkness.

I once dreamed the Sun and Blue Sky fell in love with the Chicagoans.

The Chicagoans were great-spirited—they honoured themselves in erecting the monument to the liberator, Lincoln, over in the beautiful Lincoln Park; they hesitated with the impulse to rest from their labours and be sentimental—to worship the lovely. Then the Sun and Blue Sky, with the best appearance and freshest sentiment, showed their sweetest attachment to the Chicagoans. What did the Sun and Blue Sky whisper to them? They so tenderly whispered to leave the city of business and dusts; they softly commanded to be a poet. The god of Chicago—or it might be a devil—was eavesdropping and overheard the whispering of the lovers. He became enraged and wildly exclaimed to the Sun and Blue Sky: "Keep away from the Chicagoans! That's not your business." Then the god—or the devil—built the forest of chimneys, burned the soft coal, because it is the cheapest, and bade all the chimneys to blow up all the smokes like volcanoes. All the chimneys obeyed his command. The result was tragic, since the Sun and the Blue Sky, being separated by the smoke, lost all chances to see the Chicagoans. The Master of Chicago gave a final command to the Chicagoans: "You must be satisfied with the city of business; you ought to marry with Money and Smoke." This was my dream.

Chicago is Chicago only because he has the smoke. Without it Chicago would lose his character, although it is an unpleasant character. I rather would have even a bad character than to have none.

Smoke! "Smoke" means Chicago as "flower" means Japan. Money! "Money" means Chicago as "art" means Japan. There's some difference, you see, between Chicago and Japan.

I tell you, my friend Chicagoan, you will turn to a negro if you do not beware, living in such a smoke. If you could turn wholly to a black, gaining his gentle, merry spirit with his skin, that would be far better than to remain as a white-faced human machine in crazy Chicago. The negroes are harmless, happy, the most obliging creatures in the world; the negro is an ignorant, optimistic poet, in fact. Thank God they are not "educated!" With knowledge of book and world no one can be jolly. That the wise man generally is not fat, with the happy smile and the jolly humour, is the rule.

The negroes have the simplest child heart; they have a warm love of a variety of loud colours. I saw almost every day a negro on the streets of San Francisco who carried proudly a silver-tipped cane in his right hand with the jaunty air of a cake-walk artist. How brightly sparkled a diamond pin on his red necktie! What a combination, red with his black face! Was it a real diamond? Of course, with the negro of America, as with anybody elsewhere, all that sparkles is not diamond. The negroes are delighted with all that glitters, and they are not particular enough to distinguish between sham gems and real.

I see many negroes in Chicago who are not dressed with loud colours and sparkling stones. Perhaps the negroes of the Pacific coast are more richly situated. The negro of San Francisco I am speaking of wore a yellow vest and blue trousers; his shoes were tan. I hear that one of your great council districts is represented by a statesman of like tastes—the Honourable Coughlin, is it not?

Did you ever hear the negro crying? I suppose not. They were born with only laughter, though the other fellows learned first to cry, their laughter coming later. The negroes are the most wonderful mortals with overflowing humour. The humour of their manner, the humour in their voice, the humour in every part of their bodies makes us think of every one of them as a comic actor. Glad am I to have acquaintance with a few negro gentlemen. Is there any reason why they cannot be gentlemen being waiters? What are their names? Who knows?

Seeing me every morning they cordially welcome me with silent large smiles, showing me their white teeth, sparkling their somewhat yellow eyes. Their graceful manner and gentility soon make me forget anything unagreeable about them and bring me to a fairy world of sweetness and satisfaction. I can not be happy unless waited on by some black face. I recall what a jolly face they make when they find a "two-bits" under the plate. Oh, happy negro gentleman-waiter! I love you. I will be with you forever!

One morning I paid for my breakfast with a five-dollar piece of gold—do you know that in California only the gold is acceptable money? Such a solid green piece of paper ought to go into the waste basket. Paper money? What a value is in it, anyhow? How can I distinguish a counterfeit from the real money? You say there is no counterfeit in Chicago?

"That's not money; take it away—destroy it," I said when the black waiter—such a jolly gentleman negro—gave me a dirty green paper as a change for my gold piece.

He laughed, showing his ivory teeth like a gentle bear, and said with lovely excitement:

"You are all right. Throw it away if you wish, but—I will pick it up and keep it myself. Ha, ha, ha!" He laughed like thundering.

Even a soiled paper is worth something, no doubt, in America.

But the trouble is, to keep such a paper makes the pocket awfully wet. Need not keep it, spend it, you say? All right, my dear sir; Chicago makes that easy, if not pleasant.

O negroes, you good-natured, never-getting-sad creatures! I am all ready any day to leave this stone-hearted, smoky-faced city of Chicago and join with you to your native land. You have no home, you say? You were imported as a slave many a year ago, you say? Slave! What a sadly sweet submitting, what a gently melancholy obedience the word "slave" expresses! You were perfectly fortunate that you were slave; the people who kept you as slave were greatly mistaken. I see still some stains of slavery in your face, as I can recognise the traces of nobility in the face of a bridge beggar who was once a noble man. Surely you have had a sad experience.

Chicago is the city of "no time to spare for another;" Chicago is the city of "time is money;" Chicago never invites any lazy guest; Chicago has no patience for the people asking questions, moving uncertainly—although I understand the patience of American gentlemen, especially for ladies, is perfectly angelic, waiting upon them without complaining, but with the highest satisfaction and good humour. Chicago never tastes of peaceful harmony and complete leisure, consequently he cares nothing for a man of quiet thought and slow steps, but he loves a bright young man. What does he care for any old crippled tramp?

The great city of Chicago is very cruel; he may drown any man, whom he sees unnecessary in the city, in the Lake of Michigan, as the cider-presser throws away the useless stuff after taking the juice out of the apple. The man whom Chicago respects must be a crazy man, rushing on like a racehorse, wide awake, like an alarm clock.

Chicago is not the city of gentlemen. What do I mean by "gentleman," you say? Chicago is the city of the sack coat, if I can say that Washington is the city of the dress coat and Boston is the city of the frock coat. The sack-coat city of Chicago has not enough dignity to attend with proper ceremony upon a high-born lady, or to conduct suitably the funeral of a great general. What a pity—such mighty strength, so little restraint or cultivation! Chicago himself, perhaps, does not care to attend to these affairs. Chicago, I think, wants to be an eternal sack-coat city. Chicago wants to be far away from the conventional society of foolish display or stupid formality. Chicago wants simply to mind his own business—that is, to make money, to build the highest building in the world, and to keep a lady in leisure. Is she satisfied in leisure? Not a bit! How unwise she is! She wants to leave the home and engage in the trade of the street and the mart like the men.

The great dream of Chicago is to invent a machine that will kill 10,000 hogs a minute. Chicago cannot, with his present aims and ambitions, ever become a high-minded city.

"Mind your own business!" It is the most typical maxim of Americans. If you rightly understand it, you are on the road of success and glory in this world. "Mind your own business" means "taking care only of myself," does it not?

There are many in Chicago who so understand it, if I am not mistaken. The people in the street, I mean, especially. They are so unkind, impolite, rough. They only take care of themselves; they cannot spare even a minute for another's sake. If you happen to ask a question of the people in the street, they surely make a disagreeable frown before your face, and then may even murmur: "Great bore! I have no time for you."

In America—I mean in Chicago—everybody ought to know everything. Even a baby must walk alone without a nurse. The conductor never stops a car if he sees a cripple on the track. "I mind my own business; I cannot take care of you," the Chicagoans might say.

Chicago is such a hard city for the stranger—like I am. Beware, my dear stupid visitors to the city. Even to ask a slight question of the rushing people on the street is certainly something very rude. How can I, spending only a week or so, understand everything? I am not bright enough, like Chicago people, to know everything without asking.

One morning I asked a man on the street where is So-and-So street, what car to take. When I heard him murmur something I saw him already one hundred yards away from me. Is that the way to treat a little Oriental? I felt so indignant. I asked the same question of another man. The man said coldly: "No time now, you ask somebody else." I was almost crying, do you know? I remember that a San Francisco lady said at my departure that I will be lost in the great city of Chicago. Yes, my dearest sweet woman on the Pacific coast, I will surely be lost!

The third gentleman I asked was a rather fat young man in a handsome suit. I thought him very well-bred, having a tender sympathy for a stranger and a fine heart. Did he answer me nicely, you say? No. He said roughly: "Go to a policeman!"

"Oh, policeman, where are you?" I exclaimed.

I hurried to a book printer's and got a book of street guides of this city of Chicago. "Now, I am all right!" I said with great joy. "I thank you much, dear guide maker; you gave relief to a stupid Oriental gentleman."

Yes, I think the god of the Chicagoans is a devil.

III

WITHIN THE EVENING SKY IS the star; behind the book the man; in the city of Chicago the wealth and thundering noise. Not only in the streets—the true thunders often verily roar over Chicago. Even God makes some joy in the great, crazy city, as it seems to me, adding more noisy demonstrations to the already unbearable trumpets of Chicago. The most noisy time in the world is the time of highest human energy and excitement. The night is quiet, the night is when the human energy and excitement sleep in silent lullaby of stars and soft kissing of breeze. Human beings—even nature or God—find it impossible to explain their power and motion without making noise. See how the oceans roll, how the Yosemite shouts, how the overland trains rush! See the clamorous crowd at the fruit market by the Chicago River!

Chicago is the noisiest city in America! Doesn't this mean that Chicago is the city with the highest human energy and greatest excitement in America? Doesn't it mean that Chicago is the most successful city of worldliness and "go-aheadism?" Worldliness and "go-aheadism" are measured by the amount of noise.

You, poet who prefers a rose petal to the Masonic Temple, need not stay in Chicago even a minute. Do you cover your ears against the threatening dins of the city? Do you close your eyes against the endless procession of rushing people? Some, stumbling, throw away the gold and make a sad face—what a pity! You go away from Chicago into the wood, and dream by the rivulet. You are undoubtedly familiar with the cadence and feeling of wood, and rivulet, but you are too simple-minded to understand the confused human sound of the city; the great drama of tears and laughter acted daily on the big stage of Chicago is too much for your childish heart. Chicago is not the city to take care particularly of children, as is Japan. But if you wish to stay, you may; Chicago is indifferent. If you wish to go, you go. Chicago is as big as the Lake of Michigan, and Chicago is cold as a jail.

"Chicago? That's American!" I exclaimed. "That's American" means great, as "that's German" means steady, and "that's French" means artistic, and "that's English" means comfortable, and "that's Japanese" means dainty, and "that's Chinese" means gross. You ask me what I mean by "great?" Chicago is America. America without Chicago would lose what is America.

If there be the time when we complain that the world is small, America will be as large as she is today, and the Americans immense forever. If there be the time when we will complain that America is small, Chicago will be as large as today, and the Chicagoans immense forever. I hail you—Chicago!

Are you really only sixty years old, my dearest Chicago? Sixty years are merely a short hour. "You tell a lie, you rather-old-looking City of Men!" I declared often. How can anything under the sun grow so fast? Chicago himself says: "I live in hard working and in darkest smoke, naturally I get rugged and tired; very likely I look older than my own age."

I myself, being such a fellow as never kept a book in my life—even a copy of my own publications—hurried to the city library to find out the true age of Chicago. City library! After all, it cannot be anything but Chicagoesque. His is the richest library, no doubt, as everything in Chicago is great in size and wealth. Its million books are filling all the shelves, as the dry goods fill the big stores. Oh, librarian, you furnished me a very good dinner, even ice cream, but—where is the table? The Chicago city library has no solemnly quiet, softly peaceful reading-room; you are like a god who made a perfect man and forgot to put in the soul; the books are worth nothing without having a sweet corner and plenty of time, as the man is nothing without soul. Throw those books away, if you don't have a perfect reading-room! Dinner is useless without a table. I want to read a book as a scholar, as I want to eat a dinner as a gentleman. What difference is there, my dearest Chicago, between your honourable library and the great department store, an emporium where people buy things without a moment of selection, like a busy honey bee?

The library is situated in the most annoyingly noisy business quarter, under the overhanging smoke, in the nearest reach of the engine bells of the lakeside. One can hardly spend an hour in it if he be not a Chicagoan who was born without taste of the fresh air and blue sky. The heavy, oppressive, ill-smelling air of Chicago almost kills me sometimes. What a foolishness and absurdity of the city administrators to build the office of learning in such a place of restaurants and barber shops!

Look at that edifice of the city library! Look at that white marble! That's great, admirable; that means tremendous power of money. But what a vulgarity, stupid taste, outward display, what an entire lacking of fine sentiment and artistic love! Ah, those decorations with gold and green on the marble stone spoil the beauty! What a shame! That is exactly Chicagoesque. O Chicago, you have fine taste, haven't you?

The *Encyclopædia Britannica* informs that the organisation of Chicago began in the year 1837. To be exact, he is just sixty-three years old. Isn't he a wonderful young city? How can I believe that in only sixty-three years 77,000 acres, extending over fifteen miles north and south and over eight miles east and west, were occupied by 2,000,000 of people? It is magic. It grew in one night, like a spring bamboo shoot. It is like the eternal Fuji Mountain of far-off Japan, which appeared suddenly one morning 2000 years ago, as the legend tells, to the great wonder of the people. It is a dream. It is just like a story.

You ought to know whom you talk to before you speak. Chicago is almost a baby city, as far as its age concerns, for there are many cities a thousand years old in this world. Is it natural and right for you to want the baby city to be poetical, to be philosophical at once? You, who are complaining to Chicago of its lacking of profound refinement and gentle manners, are foolish as much as one who wants a baby to reply to the greatest questions of life and death. You must give time—one hundred years or two hundred perhaps—to Chicago. The grandchildren of Chicago will learn surely how to speak to strangers, what is art, how to spell correctly the names of great poets.

How painful and unpleasant to see the precocious young philosophers or poets whose faces are pale, whose sad eyes are downcast! Young men should be young men; they should laugh with the world and sunshine; they should work hard like the summer ants; they should be hopeful as a spring morn. Glad am I to be acquainted with this great city of Chicago. Chicago is the typical city of modern young men. Chicagoans take the world straight, give to the world a plain statement; Chicagoans never understand the world in cynical ways or dreamy fashions. They take the world in all-roundly good process and with fine understanding; they are happy, no doubt; they are glad to live and work. They eat plenty meats at morning; they work hard in daytime; they play ball on Sunday. Look at their great muscles! Isn't it simply grand?

It is such a refreshment for an Oriental like me to meet with Chicagoans. I feel myself the new blood of modern life and freshest joy of the world circulating in me, and I am almost come to exclaim: "Oh, empty dreams and visionary poems, go away from me! I am to be a plain modern youth of the world of money and happiness. How glad to be a fine materialist! What a joy to be a hard worker! Work means growing hope and new sunshine."

Nearly all the Chicagoans, except but one or two mortals with the subtitle poet, are fine materialists—notice that adjective "fine." They are born hard workers; laziness is truly an unpardonable crime to them. They are proud any time to show their big muscles of arms, like hams, and their broad shoulders, like the branches of the redwood under the severe force of winter. Chicago never allows any do-nothing fellow to come up here; the shiftless, lazy dude, whose only care is to perfect the curve of his finger nails, knocks at the gate of Chicago without having any answer.

I thank God, the wise, most practical Chicago has not a simply handsome, good-for-nothing type of youth hanging around the cigar stores, as in San Francisco. The Chicago boys are not handsome enough to stand exposing their vain faces with the air of the perfectly superior lady killer. The Chicago boys have not such a blue eye as the San Franciscans have—Chicago herself scarcely sees the blue sky; they don't spend much money on their neckties. Those rubbish, those professional lady killers, to speak more clearly, at the cigar stand of San Francisco, with the powder on face, with the huge cane in arm, with a cigar in mouth, make the most despicable, cheapest show in the world. I advise you, my dear California, to pass a law suppressing them. They are a great disgrace to your honourable State.

Thank heaven, the Chicago cigar stores are not fitted for the convenience of such hangerson. But I am sorry that I, myself enjoying sometimes a cigarette, can hardly find a good one in Chicago. Worst of all, is that any cigar store north of the river does not keep even a bad cigarette. Still, I do not miss the smoke here as one would do in another city; one has but to breathe in the air. I am sorry that the Chicago cigar store does not have a slot machine. What a disappointment! I cannot try a fortune by dropping a nickel.

How can Chicago take care of sick people? Chicago might say: "I am not a hospital." Chicago has no tenderness of the grandmother, Chicago is taking always the unchangeable attitude of the cold business man. Chicago is the city of wheat and of pork. Think just a moment of 2,000,000 of Chicagoans, with the strongest nerve force and vigorous, regular action of the stomach and clean blood in quick circulation! I know that the doctors have a hard struggle in this great city. I do not observe here so many signs of doctors as I did on the Pacific coast. But I am not sure of the business of lawyer.

I observed that the Chicago people, especially I mean the people on the street, do not wear much of white shirts. Laundry work of Chicago is not good, I understand. The Chicagoans are not dudes, but the most honest, simple, working men. When I left San Francisco nearly all the San Francisco gentlemen wore, as I observed, the black stiff hat of $3.50, and in Chicago I observe that they do not sacrifice much money in their headgear. Some of the Chicagoans wear a straw hat of $1, some a cap of half a dollar, some a rather cheap, black, stiff hat, some a grey soft one. They wear such stuff with perfect satisfaction, because these things are cheap, but not because a cheap thing is more appropriate or becoming in the weather of Chicago. I saw only one or two gentlemen in silk hats, except the carriage drivers, since I was in Chicago. The silk hat does not fit with the city's sack coat. Perhaps it is because the lawyers, doctors, or the honourable judges of this great city want to be distinguished from the driver.

IV

ONE DAY I PRESENTED TO Chicago a cotton handkerchief of enormous size, with the red flowers as decorations, and one silk, but very tiny one, requiring him to prefer one of them. Chicago was not bright enough to imagine vividly that I was examining his own character. Chicago is gentle, sometimes so stupid, and it is well that he is so, since such is the general character of the most practical person. Chicago is not the city with wolfish teeth and hawk eye, like a thief. He is a plain, big city of good-natured America, oh, so slow oftentimes to discover another's secret scheme. He is too large-hearted, sometimes ridiculously so, to appreciate anything.

Now to return to the handkerchief business. Which was Chicago's selection? Chicago chose the former—that is, the cotton handkerchief of enormous size. Chicago has no secret; never tells a lie, I presume. Chicago's heart opens wide to anybody without a screen or door, like the art gallery at the lakeside. Chicago has the frankness of children; speaks out everything like a phonograph—even something not to be spoken. Chicago is perfectly ignorant of the art of little-speaking and silence-keeping. Chicago is never still, naturally never sleeps. Chicago is the city of day, when dreams and rest have no power. Chicago is the city of clean glass which has no mystery.

Hear what Chicago said on his preference of the handkerchiefs I presented: "I take this cotton one because this is large in size and looks pretty with red flowers." What a shame! To the most practical Chicago the quality and taste of silk handkerchief are nothing of value. Chicago, eternal city without quality and taste!

Chicago is such a city who loves a penny rather than ten yards of divine poems of Heaven and rose. The Chicago poets—isn't it a surprise to be informed that certain groups of poets exist even in Chicago? How many altogether in this great Cook County, my dear sir, are starving to death, no doubt! You better be a barber or waiter rather than a well-known poet in this country—of course in Chicago. To be even a shoe-polisher, making a living in competition with black faces, is, indeed, a great deal better than to be a "lover of nature." America, or Chicago, is any day ready to offer you a laurel of "fame," but not a nickel under the sun.

The laurel of "fame" costs him nothing in the world. He does gladly send away a thousand laurels of "fame" according to order every where—today to Mr. A, and tomorrow to Mr. B, and he has forgotten whom he bestowed them upon and when. The vain poets, the most pretentious mortals who sing daily to be free from the vanity, but are verily hungry for the admiration and pompous demonstration, wear that laurel of "fame" with great satisfaction and walk around with proud gesticulations like an ostrich, after a glance in the mirror.

But look at that one who offered it to them, sneering tremendously after them behind the door. He said: "There fools, go! Your crowns are paper-made and painted." What a pity! What a poor poet! America, the cruel, money-worshipping America, may any day drive these harmless poets away from the country as Russia with the Jew people, because America with heavy purse and handsome clothes cannot endure their long, uncombed hair and thin, pale faces.

I understand that Chicago has already proclaimed against the poets. "Your being in our city means a nuisance; therefore you are to go away. Chicago is not the right place for your honourable dream and being lazy to the extreme. We hear often that all the people like you live in Boston. Do they not? Please, my dear fellows, go there!" What Boston, being also one of the American cities, is going to do with the wonderful crowd of poets, I wonder?

YONE NOGUCHI

Show me where is the beautiful lady who is our ideal! Where are the people who have no transgression, no fault and no weakness! If the Chicagoans have a blemish, as any countryman has, it must be surely that they do measure everything by its size and mere appearance. The great love of the immense size and appearance becomes a crime—perhaps not a crime, but assuredly a shame, since you discard utterly all thought of high quality and taste.

Although Chicago is the city caring only for the big size and appearance, the face of Chicago looks so dark under the thick smoke, and the appearance of Chicagoans in the ill-fitting suits is pitiful. Chicago keeps saying: "Any old piece will do, if its size is large and it looks good." That is the unmovable principle of Chicago. Size! Appearance! Not the quality, not the taste!

How can Chicago attain to the highest dignity? How can he procure a true admiration from the thoughtful critics? Does he not care for the criticism by others? Is he unconventional? My dear sirs, I have never encountered with such a conventional people in my life as the Americans—as the Chicagoans, if your prefer—who are astonishingly sensitive to any criticism. They are like a snail—merely one touch of the finger makes their whole construction shudder as by a storm. But they are giant in body like an elephant; don't you know that the elephant is the most sensitive of animals?

I perfectly understand why newspaper-cutting bureaus are making a solid business in this country. They are securing bread and butter, I conclude, out of the foolishness of people, the vain wishes to hear what praise another has given. The Americans are so childishly honest—is honest the right word? They would gladly accept every good word spoken to them with straight doubtlessness, without any discrimination. What pitifully blind people who are so fatally unable to distinguish between flattery and the true praise! I value highly, however, the most gentle quality in Americans that never allows any suspicion of another's word. They are perfect angels in such matters. Really they will paste in their scrapbooks even a senseless babbling of a baby if it was concerned with them, and they will keep it in the safe. Scrapbook has an equal estimation to them as an heirloom, or diamond ring of grandmother.

If you will declare that the Chicagoans are ridiculous, that exactly means to put a verdict of "ridiculous" on the heads of Americans. The Chicagoans who incessantly keep saying: "Look, just a moment; look, my dear visitor; am I not beautiful? How do you think of me? Please, say I am good looking!"—as a dear little butterfly girl with red ribbon and straw hat—are verily ridiculous, are they not? To tell the truth, I was sickly tired in California with such a stupid, tasteless-like-wax, nonsensical question as, "How do you like America?" or "How long have you been?" Not because I have no correct answers, but truly because my sincere reply might make my interview tragic.

I tried so far to keep myself from being introduced to new people, simply because I hated to come face to face with such an eternal stereotyped question. And, alas, I found myself in the same ditch in this Chicago! Oh, how many commonplace encounters I had with the everlasting "How do you like Chicago?" and "How long do you expect to stay?" I almost decided to have my answers printed on paper and to show it before my new acquaintance began to throw the questions over me.

What opinion I have of Chicago? Shall I flatter? The Chicagoans will make a somewhat awkward, smiling face—and look with the twinkling eyes of satisfaction and conceit of "I expect so." And they will say in slow, haughty tones: "This is the most great city—don't you know?" Shall I speak my true opinion? How my interview will end?

I must be a hermit in Chicago, although I have a heavy mission to investigate this big man-town. Why? Because I have no more desire to make enemies personally than to make more friends. Personal disagreement or quarrel is the most sad experiment. As for me, I have a proud, hard-to-bend backbone. I was born without flattery or sycophancy. I find it more difficult to please the Americans than to graduate from the University of Chicago. Yes, sir; I am too honest for the Americans—for the Chicagoans, if you please!

You, my dear Chicago people, don't come approaching me with the bothering questions on Chicago and the Chicagoans, but softly, gracefully step towards me, as your sweet summer evening breeze, with the much beautiful chat of divine star or angel rose!

I really wonder whether the average Chicagoan knows how roses look! Do you know, Chicagoan, that roses don't grow on the mountain top or in the river?

To say too much with almost any matter is far from to be admirable. The Tokio servant girls are despised, simply because they talk silly nonsense hanging around the public well with water bucket in hand. Chattering is an offence in Japan, the land of pride and peace.

YONE NOGUCHI

I am stopping now with my criticism on Chicago and the Chicagoans. To stop means to save my dignity. A poet ought to be silent. Was I of service to you, my dear friend? I pray that you will fully appreciate my frankness. Good-bye! May nothing worse befall you!

My First London Experience (1903)

My art of making myself at home even in an impossible place, which my long sojourn in lands strange and new taught me, alas! in spite of myself, seemed to fail flatly in London. I thought she (more likely London is he), like Japan of many temperaments, had been indulging herself in bad humour, perhaps in sorrow of reminiscence on the August passed, or perhaps in chronic fear of coming winter, as the month of my arrival was November. I stood silent in thought that my slight movement of affection might make her more disagreeable; I kept at a distance as much as I could. I slowly felt that I was out of place, when I imagined a certain hostility between myself and London. I was so sorry in leaving Boston, and even New York, until one day when, long after my hunt for a hidden affinity which I fancied I might discover in the rôle of sightseer, had ended, everything changed at once: London, the greatest city of the world, at last turned her interesting face to me. And, after a Western fashion, I kissed her. We became one. Let me tell you how I found her beauty.

It was about four o'clock, or earlier than that, of one day in the month of December. I always feel curious, and even ambitious, about that hour, as there is some time yet before supper, and I feel as if my day's work was done. I was standing on Westminster Bridge, but not without a reason; as it was the "pea-soup day," London's mental attitude, I thought, was quite dubious. How I complained of the fact that she was sticking too close to her own senses (also to the earth); how I wished even once she could act fantastically. Her geographical transcendency looked now to me extremely poetical, though not verily beautiful; it is my opinion the real poetry has to do only a little with beauty. I was almost in a delirium or dream (here standing on the bridge perfectly sieged by the greyness of fog), where neither latitude nor longitude bothered me; the only difference between me and the doves that swarmed around me on the most intimate terms was that I could not fly. It was, indeed, the first time that the old soul of London even appeared to flirt with me through the almost frivolous sway of those doves' wings. I was much pleased with it. The fogs hid the ugly sign of a certain drink on the other side; the audacities of Cleopatra's Needle that often made me uncertain at once calmed down in a graceful way unimaginable. I raised my head, and alas, observed to my great surprise two unusually large suns in real old gold, in the East and West, on both sides of the bridge where, as I said, I had to have a little talk with the doves. I was glad to say that the thing of wonder appeared by magic at last in London. I would not listen, I decided, if anybody might say that one of the red balls on the lower skies was but the moon. Under my feet Thames stopped running down. "What a picture!" I exclaimed. "Oh, what fogs!"

Joaquin Miller, my old California friend, often told me that I would best avoid the word of fog in poetry; he even inclined to call Poe vulgar from only that one point of his frequent use of it. But Miller's beloved word "mist" with, as it always seems to me, lightness of spring, was hardly the word I could substitute in the place of London fogs which swim, even jump, almost like a whale of fantastic shape. It was only in those days of fogs when London was pleased to be lost in the grey vastness of mystery that I could speculate on my poetical feeling; I confess that I doubted at the beginning of my arrival on the real relation of the city with Keats or Tennyson, as the people here appeared not to speak the language of either of them. I felt uneasy in mind, as my American accent might become the cause of their laughter, although, with Professor Mathews or somebody, I believe that Americans speak a far purer English than the Englishmen themselves. "Where's English poetry?" I not once exclaimed, more or less in condemnation. Happy to be a foreigner sometimes, as he can say anything he wishes, without feeling any responsibility for the creation of a condition he is going to criticize. With that right of the foreigner, I openly expressed my displeasure with London's commercialism, which verily often in the months of winter becomes, glad to say, less forcible, and even attractive, under the veil of fogs. How often I walked by the Embankment in such days or nights with all the justification of my poetical feeling; it is the sadness of the age that we must have a reason even for poetry. As I remember rightly, it was after eight or nine o'clock when I left the house of D——, Esquire, where I had gone to drink a social cup of tea; oh, it was such a foggy night when the 'buses stopped, and I wrote:

> *"Alas! I have lost my path! Astray!*
> *O cheating elf, leave me alone, pray!*
> *I long to steal toward a flowery dale by the moonbeams."*

The sad part was that, not reaching the flowery dale, I stepped out on to Westminster Bridge, long after my groping by the walls of Buckingham Palace and many other places; it was almost midnight when I reached my lodgings in Brixton Road, at one pound a week, cold and fireless. I was then only a little better off than my friend Yoshio Markino, with whom I lived; not better off in money, but in the fact that I had a letter of praise in my drawer written by Meredith. I am sure I should become mad and despise London for such almost impossible fogs if I were an Englishman; but let me say once for all that it was the illogicalness of a foreigner (What? Delightful quality, is it?) that made me love her much more for her faults. How pleasing to stand above the usual common senses native to the land! I had been leading such a life here and there for more than ten years.

I do not quarrel with the Englishmen when they hate the fogs; but I should like to impress on them their strange beauty. It is altogether their prejudice, not their blindness, not to sing them in poetry, paint them in picture; I feel much pleased to speculate on the possible effect of even Markino's pictures of fog, although they might be unsatisfactory to you, and think that they might open their eyes to the fogs without the appreciation of which these months of London's winter would be sadder than total blank. I often thought of the London fogs as of a great artistic problem (why not?); they might stand in the same relation as *tsuyu*, or rainy season, for us Japanese. The beauty of the fogs can only appeal to one whose æstheticism is older than life; their grey effect is a far more living thing than darkness or death. What a world of twilight, where your dream and reality shall be joined by one long sorrow of Eternity! What a song of greyness, which is the highest! What an atmosphere by whose magic you shall find slowly a mysterious way to your ideal. It is one month of rain that makes Japanese reflective, teaches them a lesson of patience, while the fogs turn Englishmen, the most unpoetical of people, even poetical, accepting the theory that poetry is a criticism of life. It is again by reason of the mental effect they receive from them that they cannot leave poetry alone. Both of them, rain and fogs, force us within the door, and result in making us home people; it is true, I think, we would not have conceived such an elaborate way of making tea or arranging flowers, if we did not have the rainy season; and without the winter of fogs, the English people would be less bright in conversation, and the delightfulness of the English drawing-room would be less complete. Indeed, for the existence of the society and the club in England the fogs should be thanked. Who will say they are disagreeable? I believe that what I have said here is not merely a psychological speculation.

It is not too much to say that there is no country like England, where people show their best at afternoon tea; while the talk of gentlemen is always effective, the silence of the ladies is far more effective. (It reminds me that the voice is silver and silence gold.) The topics they talk on are various, the differences in opinion being well arranged, like corals on a string, of freedom which runs indeed through all the souls of them; and their having no formalism is most delightful for us Japanese, who enslave ourselves more or less under its tyranny. Such is one of the distinguished English characteristics in private and in public; publicly, I have seen it in the combat of the Press, and, more pleasing to say, at Hyde Park Corner, where Socialists, nay, even Anarchists, have equal liberty with theologians. You would not blame me if I call it the Japanese Government's most barbarous *coup d'état*, when I reflect, while I write this article, on the fact that a certain Japanese publisher was obliged to erase off the whole chapter on Socialism from his Encyclopædia, as the Government was afraid of its influence on the country. What a pity she is mistaken in thinking oppression necessary to the keeping of perfect order! I am sure that not only the foreigners, but the Englishmen, too, feel very little the officialism of London; and I have many reasons to believe, with many other Japanese, that England is the most comfortable country of the world to live in. How can you find her otherwise, when our right is well respected, and we are treated with much consideration? She is the country where (now returning to the English drawing-room) you will be asked, "One lump or two lumps?" And again she is the country where you can take sugar as many lumps as you wish. I thank the English ladies who always gave me a comfortable corner of their drawing-rooms, where I could freely indulge in my habitual silence even amid their talk; how delightful it was to watch the profiles of people which suddenly visualised themselves through the fragrance of smoke. I will never forget how beautifully the Lady C—— smoked; what a charm in her little fingers! What a fair skin was hers! It may have been the famous English skin, famous all over the world. And what audacity, almost sportsmanlike, when she asked her lady friend at her departure, "Take a little whisky, dear, before you go?"

It is admirable of them to believe that England is the first country of the world, and that Englishmen are the recognised protectors of civilisation and peace, and they act accordingly; such a belief of theirs could be clearly seen, I often thought, in the fact that they never asked me, as Americans would, what I thought of England and her people. They smiled with no particular reason when I expressed my wonder at the bigness of London, which is not even a little stirred by the footstep of a poet-writer, as the said Lady C—— rather bluntly put it when I disclosed my poetical ambition. Without any bitterness toward her, although I confess a little discouragement at her words then, I decided to bring out a sixteen-page pamphlet with my own money, some three pounds which I had kept aside for the purpose of two days in Paris at Christmas. When I got some proof of my success in my poetical adventure, I wrote to dear old Stoddard of Hawaiian fame, the true friend of Stevenson, to whom I dedicated *From the Eastern Sea*, who answered me in the following fashion:

"O my poet! Can you imagine my surprise when I turned the leaves of your latest book, and found it was dedicated to me? I was quite wild with excitement; I hardly knew what to do with myself. Oh, I am so happy! Your success is now assured in England. The moment you are recognised by the right person, or persons, you are recognised by all the London world. Now, you see, like my Lord Byron, you wake up to find yourself famous! O, my beloved kid, I am so glad—so very, very glad!"

Dear old emotional Stoddard! While I was not sure of my awakening like Byron, I confessed I was not without pleasure then at being spoken of in such style. The main point is to impress on you that the true soul of London, at least her own literary soul, is not proportionless like her measurelessly expanded streets; indeed, she is moved by the guidance of a few right persons. Great London, who looked so cold and unsympathetic at the beginning, began to smile toward me quite passionately; I even sang a love song into her ears.

It would look a sort of note of a common traveller to write generally on the British Museum or the National Gallery; beside, it is not light work by any means. One strong impression I received in the former place was when I turned the leaves of Blake's large hand-illuminated book; how strengthened my mind grew from seeing the living proof of art greater than life. And again it was in the same place that I felt an almost reverent thrill when I saw Sir D——, already old as he was, but young and single-minded, studying the forgotten Chinese book with such a zeal; I wished to disappear on the spot when he insisted on my enlightening his mind on a certain phrase in the book, as he thought, doubtless, I might be quite a Chinese scholar. In fact, it is only lately that I began, shame to say, my own study of the Orient.

How often I went to the National Gallery, particularly in Turner's Rooms, before London's drawing-rooms opened their social doors for me, sometimes with my friend Markino, more often with my imaginary person, artist or critic, to whom I could talk, as much as I wanted, on Turner. I was very glad that I had resisted the temptation of Ruskin's books beforehand, as I wished to see Turner with my own eyes. The favourite talk between me and my imaginary person, perhaps an Englishman, was on the arts subjective and objective; I tried hard to impress him with the importance of the Oriental conception of art, by that I mean the subjective. When I went so far as even to point out Turner's technical fault (now looking at his biggest canvas in the room), and, for argument's sake, called him a subjective artist, even emphasizing that he was most Oriental in heart, he would exclaim at once: "Admitting these faults as you wish, what then? Don't they make a great service to the whole canvas as a relief? Look at those masts, if you please! And again at those smokes! How perfect in technique! What I see most in it is the mighty glory of the master technician. Isn't it great that any portion of his picture, supposed to be torn out, can make a complete picture by itself?" He appeared to be pleased when I agreed to go carefully, beginning with technique in his water-colours; but it seemed he did not listen at all to my words of denunciation with his too wonderful colour not quite true to nature. I was sorry, however, he did not see that my real point in denying his technical magic was to value more his imagination and impulse, and more the real colour behind his pictures which was a song and passion.

I cannot pass without a word on the Tate Gallery, particularly Rossetti's pictures in it, which served most mysteriously to make me understand his poems better; I am not playing a paradox in saying that his unnaturalness was most natural, his formalism a living fire itself. It was partly Rossetti's memory, the existence of Carlyle's house of course, that often turned my head toward Chelsea; but it is more true to say that my main reason was to feel a strangely mingled impression of the city and country there. As I have a proverb, "A good man loves a mountain, while a wise man water," it is easy to associate Carlyle with Chelsea;

but I would never believe, if I had not been told, that Keats wrote *To a Nightingale* here. It should be Hampstead, "not far from man, verily near to God," for him. I confess I could not believe, though without any strong reason for my disbelief, that George du Maurier was lying there. However, he would feel particularly uncomfortable, I thought, as it was not that Immortal Bird we hear nowadays at Hampstead, but the thrush, which might be a better subject for the pages of *Punch*. It was here on a certain afternoon in the month of March that I smelled first the most keen fragrance of violets, as keen as any ode of Keats'. I thought that England's winter was nearly over, and it was about the time when London was going to put away her grey cloak like that of Hamlet. Sad to say, I was obliged to leave London before the purple gossamers had begun to veil over Hyde Park. I could not offer my respect to Disraeli on Primrose Day; one of his novels, though I forget its title, was the first English novel ever I got in my boyhood day with money from my peddling Japanese colour-prints in the streets of San Francisco.

Let me read the first part of my own English diary at random, as I like to feel the old sensation again afresh:

Nov. 2nd

Hoity-toity! Is this London really? "That is too sudden," I exclaimed. All my friends over the seas, the curtain has risen at last; the play is now beginning.

'Buses and again 'buses! Cabs and again cabs! What a crowd! How dirty are those streets! I am glad not to see any dog around here, whom I always hate. But isn't it a pity that the English girls wear rather shabby hats? The gentlemen look to play with their own dignity. I have not seen even one gentleman who is fat and jolly; I see that it would be taken here as a crime to look happy. I am often told that we must see the Englishman at home, if we wish to see him at his best. That may be true.

I felt already influenced by the English atmosphere silent and solemn, even before a few hours had hardly passed. I almost forgot, under such an influence, how to speak.

I never saw before such tired-looking people who filled the hotel lobby; they may be, like myself, foreigners who have come to see London. I should like to know their first impression here.

Ladies and gentlemen, where is famous St. Paul's Cathedral? Didn't I expect to see it from any corner? I wished in my heart an evening bell would sing out from Westminster Abbey, when I stepped into London.

Oh, where is the London Bridge? I will dust my hat, and go out to dine somewhere, and study a bit London by night.

I ate a "grilled chop" last night. My friends in America, do you ever know what is a "lemon squash?" Is there no water in London? The waiter looked strangely at me when I asked after it; why, I forgot this was England, where are only two things, beer and Bible.

I believe the word economy is the keynote of English greatness. Let me learn it (what a great problem) beginning with one pitcher of water, with which I have to be content for my morning toilet. Indeed, I wish to have bath-houses rather than the statues I encounter here at almost every corner; I see that you have to begin with hero-worship in England, while cleaning your body is the first thing in Japan.

"Biscuit, sir," the waiter says when I ask for crackers. Any name will do as long as the thing is the same. Let me get a copy of the book, *How to Act in London*.

I have the most unhappy breakfast at this hotel; it would be better, I thought, to eat even alone in any big temple. The air in the hotel is cold; the dining-room reminds me of a drawing-room of an American undertaker.

What a parade of frock coats! I never saw before such a crowd of men in that coat; the frock coat will be eternally unchanged and the same, however the world might change, or an Imperial Kingdom turn to a republic. How many hundred thousand people in that immortal coat pass by Charing Cross every day? It is here that I wrote one seventeen syllable *hokku* poem, which appears, when translated, as follows:

"Tell me the street to Heaven.
This? Or that? Oh, which?
What webs of streets!"

Today I rode on a 'bus, taking a "garden seat," from which I could command a general view over the streets; what a human desert under my feet, groaning monotonous and sad! The air above my head was clear. The driver touched the horses lightly, and tried to encourage them with the hum of song. Oh, where did I wish to go? I did not know, to be sure. And how could I know since the London streets were a perfect puzzle? The horses stopped. I left the 'bus before I had any thought. Somebody said to me: "This is the place where Johnson, Boswell, too, used to walk in ancient day, and they laughed, talked, and ate beefsteak pie to heart's content." Why, this was Temple Bar.

6th

I wrote to my friend in America that the price of champagne was delightfully cheap. I was much pleased to buy chestnuts in the street, an excusable taste, considering their price. But I am very sorry that I cannot give any good word to coffee here; I am learning to drink tea even at breakfast. A healthy symptom of Englishmen can be seen in the amount that they eat every day; they cannot go to sleep till they eat a full supper at ten or eleven o'clock. What simplicity! I am beginning to use a pipe for my smoke, following after an English fashion.

I was pleased not to see many advertisements round the Tower of London, when I went there today. You will be inquisitive of a little handbag that I carried; you must not laugh and say something mean, if I confess I had a copy of the London guidebook in it.

Thames was black like ink. It would be on such a day as this that the ghosts of those who have been killed may appear and disappear, haunting the Tower. I was far from feeling well. I was frightened by a ghost—the ghost I made acquaintance with in the play of *Hamlet*—at a dark corner of a corridor; but it turned out in a prosaic way, since this is London, that he was nobody but a "beefeater" with many medals on his breast.

It would be better for you not to ask how famous London Bridge looked.

8th

I was caught by the rain in the street. I dropped into a tea-house. Alas! I already have a tea mania. How untidy of those English women not to try even to raise their skirts under the rain! They walked without hats, undisturbed and composed as if nothing fell from the sky. The style of shoes they wore was not satisfactory.

13th

Westminster, at last! The dear verger whom I fancied to be a spirit from any tomb in the Abbey, disappointed me when he approached me, not in Greek or Latin as I wished, but in plain English, to make me buy a guide-book of the place.

YONE NOGUCHI

It would be courteous to have the bust of Longfellow here; but I wished Washington Irving might be with him. Where is an American writer who was more loyal than he?

I saw somebody spit on Dr. Johnson's tomb. Poor old LL.D.! My imagination's ears heard his roar of revilement. Certainly, it was a too jolly nose, that of the poet Goldsmith of Ireland.

26th

I took a nap. Is it true it is said to be a proper thing to do in England? Today is Sunday. I cannot help feeling quite religious staying in London. When I stepped into St. Paul's, the service had already begun; the Bishop coughed, I should say, divinely. I walked home, that is, to the poor lodging in Brixton Road, after the service was over; the soft breeze, unusual for the season, as it was near December, kissed my brown cheeks. Thames seen from the Victoria Embankment under the darkness was not altogether unpoetical.

VI

AGAIN IN LONDON (1913–14)

I

I WAS THANKFUL THAT ENGLAND (or perhaps London) began already at the Nord Station, where my English was found to be of some use, and happier still that I could buy my beloved old *Punch* with the English money. Good-bye, francs and centimes! People in Paris must have thought me an idiot or something quite superhuman, as, when I took a 'bus or bought a picture postcard or a necktie, I had to spread out the French money in a row upon my palm and let them take whatever they liked. But at the Nord Station I felt as if I had grown into a man at once out of a childish helplessness, when I could protect my own pocket-book, and know what was in it. I surprised the French porter who carried my Japanese bamboo portmanteau to a compartment when I emptied all the French money still left in my pocket. Such a smile I tell you he smiled; oh! such a happy smile. There is only one thing that speaks a universal language—that is a smile.

I was perfectly delighted with the Nord express till I grew suddenly suspicious, exactly two hours later, at the dinner-table and asked whether I was not running by train somewhere to Chicago or Pittsburg. The people at the table were all Americans, who talked in terribly nasal voices (believe me I left Japan only fifty days ago, where people are taught to speak a language of golden silence) on the price of chickens and pigs. And goodness knows what else they talked. I left half-way through table d'hôte and hurried back to my compartment, and tried my best to dream of dear old smoky London (one says she is not as smoky as she used to be) and whom I was to meet after an absence of ten years.

The Channel was extremely rough, as I expected, and again, as I expected, I was ill. The old smiling boy (beware of the old smiling boy, all of you) came to me almost every two minutes. "Ten minutes, sir, to Dover," he eventually announced and smiled. Beware again of the old smiling boy, all of you. He came soon and announced: "Five minutes, sir, just only five minutes, sir." Why, how stupid I was, not seeing his hint for tips! I examined my purse. Alas! I had only one penny, and other money all in gold. I picked out the copper and put it in his palm and looked up into his old face, which smilingly and silently asked whether I was fooling him. Certainly, I thought, he had right to object to that one penny. Then I picked out one half sovereign, with which he played a moment with trembling fingers and then he looked up smilingly and silently to me, and then, again, smilingly and silently, at the coin. "Take it, please," I said, as I thought I had no right to make him change it to small money, because it was not a matter of buying and paying.

It was already dark when the train began to move. I felt as if something like a boa or huge serpent was crawling through the jungle. The sense of time and direction had all been lost under the heavy mantle of dark clouds or rocks. I could never think, I confess, that I was coming to the city of my dream. If I was on my way to any city at all it might be, I thought, Thompson's "City of Dreadful Night," surrounded on three sides by a horrible desert and on the fourth side by a black sea on which no ship ever came; where one's life and memory, as Thompson has it in the poem, "swoon in the tragic acts." The bare trees of the roadside against the dark sky looked as if a sentinel was guarding the pass to hell. While I was wondering where in the world I should reach, the train stopped, and my ears were at once deafened by a terrible burst of noise. I knew that I had reached London after all—the city where I was going to cast the chance of my Eastern gondola of soul against a high tide of the West.

I left the train and already I was in the Strand, where I wrote some ten years ago:

> *"My soul,*
> *A ghost from the unknown air, a fay*
> *from the mist into the mist,*
> *Strays down the torrent of life."*

The hotel which was recommended by my friend I found to be frightfully noisy. When I put down my things in the room where I was taken by the hotel attendants I determined to leave the hotel right off; and as it was on my own account, I left the price of the room at the office. I took a taxi to my friend's house. As it was a short distance the charge was less than one shilling; but I threw down half-a-crown, as I had no smaller money. I felt perfectly reckless; and I thought it was jolly to act foolishly sometimes!

The next little hotel was found to be quiet. As soon as I got in the room I took away all the Western clothes and changed to my beloved Japanese nightgown, and sought the bed at once. I put the light out, and shut my eyes, and tried to sleep—but in vain. "What use to sleep upon such an early evening, being really and truly arrived in London after ten long years?" I exclaimed. And I again dressed up in the Western clothes; and I soon found myself walking slowly towards Trafalgar Square.

My friend artist, the late Hara, used to point to his picture of the winter-night view of that square, and sadly dwell on what a failure the picture was when he thought of the subject in imagination, even from Japan. Putting aside Hara's picture, indeed the night scenery of the square would be the hardest thing to paint. Oh, what a colour in air or mist! Is it purple? or is it grey? or is it dark? What is it? "Why, it is the very colour of rubies," I exclaimed.

What an activity, what a crowd in Piccadilly Circus! Where are these people going, and what purpose have they? I wonder. I walked along the streets (I do not know what streets they were), as the other people walked. Presently I felt a terrible pain in my legs. I was walking on different roads from those of Japan. The hard pavements made my legs senseless. "Oh, where is the real ground—where the kind earth I wish to touch?" I exclaimed.

I slipped into St. James's Park. When my feet really touched the real ground I felt there was something soft underneath. "Why, green grass, even in winter here! Oh! green grass in December."

II

"OH, TELL ME, HAS LONDON changed much, do you think?"

This question had been asked a hundred times in a day ever since my feet stepped in London. Why are the Englishmen getting such a silly habit to ask questions like Americans? Changed? Only goodness knows how changed London is. I confess that I could not trust my eyes; not only my eyes, but also my ears, my nose, even my tongue. I felt I was perfectly baffled, because London of my imagination was found not existing. Indeed, those ten years (that is the years I was away from London) are long enough to make any change in the world you wish to have changed. What the biggest change I notice, do you ask me? The biggest change is that nearly all the English women are found turning into French women. In what way, you may ask me? In all sorts of ways, from their mane to their dress. They are growing so charming indeed, even a little saucy hat is perfectly becoming to them. And their little skirts make them certainly ten years younger.

And how about the men? you ask.

The men are growing Americanised. Whether it is a matter sad or happy is another question. I am glad that they are now wearing a much nicer shoe, and they are not so particular with their sticks. That is quite American. I well remember, I was much afraid, when I was here from America ten years ago, to speak before the Englishmen, because my English was not King's English, but the English which I picked up from the American prairie. Besides, I could not well understand those Englishmen's English, which sounded to me then to be something like a devil's language, with such an accent which might come from the bottom of their feet. But they speak, I find now, the English so plainly and clearly. It may be that the speaking with a Cockney emphasis might be now out of fashion; and it became, I fancy, more democratic. Democratic? Indeed, the Englishmen grew quite democratic in many other things; they stopped wearing the high hats so recklessly as they used to wear them ten years ago. That is good, too, because the high hat has truly regained now its original dignity; I should say it was the matter absurd when even a shop-boy walked down a street with a high hat like a stage comedian who lost his own cue to exist. Let me drink to the high hat's long life. It is now in the place where it should be; it only belongs to the right person.

Oh, how the streets grow Americanised. But on the other hand they have lost their own old picturesqueness, which only belonged to the truly old country. I have nothing to say against their becoming much cleaner; however, it is perfectly sad to see that they are mostly disfigured by some sort of advertisement. It is a matter certainly for congratulation that the "Underground" ceased to smell horrible. But look at those advertisements which are painted on both walls of the tunnel. Oh, if they could be replaced by flowers!

And where is my old friend the 'bus-driver, who once, quite ten years ago, frightened me by pointing out the streets where Johnson used to walk with his colleagues? Oh, where is his red, dear, large, drunken face? And where is the red handkerchief which was carelessly tied around his big neck? How I wished to sit by him upon the garden seat of the old 'bus and hear the sound when his whip clacked. Look at the auto-'bus drivers today, who wear caps fit even for a soldier. Oh, what a difference!

My imagination always saw the great fogs of London from whose dark mantle the lights would shine like a demon's eyes; I thought that it might be interesting to see the day which would pass as a night, and feel, as Dickens wrote, that Nature lived hard by and was brewing on a large scale. Who says that the fogs are growing lighter every year? Oh, what makes them so? And is not the Christmas feeling too growing rather simpler? And again on the other hand is not the religious devotion also becoming weaker?

The other day I happened to be in St. Paul's Cathedral to spend a good hour, as I made a mistake about the time of an appointment at "Ye olde Cheshire Cheese" (oh, London is the same dear old London, with this cosy little place); into the Cathedral I stole like a tired ghost or a piece of leaf fallen from the City's noise. Oh, what a difference between the within and without!

> "A sanctum of shadows where dusk-robed Solitude
> Steps from thought to thought, a breeze forgotten by
> Life and Song."

I was so glad to see quite a number of people (besides the American tourists) who sat still like a Buddha monk in meditation, doubtless in the silent communion with the invisible and holy. Was I mistaken, I thought, in my saying that the English religious feeling had been waning? To say that the Cathedral was changed would sound to you ridiculous; but it is a fact. I thought ten years ago that the glittering gold of the decoration in the interior was certainly cheap, at least to our Japanese mind; that gold that made me think less of the Cathedral has turned now to such a quite old gold, or colour of the moon upon the Indian seas. What a splendid change that is!

I left the Cathedral, and looked round, standing upon the steps, like a bird almost ready to fly. An English gentleman approached me, touching his silk hat, and said:

"Are you not in any trouble with the streets? Can I be of any service to you, sir? I believe you are the Japanese Poet who has just arrived."

Oh, to be recognised in the street even by a stranger! Did I feel much flattered? My mind at once dwelt at that moment on the sweetness of the English heart. If there is a thing that will never change, I declare, that would be the real English gentleman.

III

ONCE I SHOWED MY LITTLE daughter, five years old, an English Reader with a few fairies (or faeries, if you like); her mind of curiosity-loving could not be satisfied with my uncertain answers to her question. At the moment of my departure she pulled my sleeve of *kimono*, and looked up to my face, and said: "Papa, you must write me from London, when you see any real fairy there. I cannot read letters, but mamma will read it for me. Write me a long letter about the fairy if she ever spoke to you in London streets."

What have I to write my daughter now, when I saw one at the Lyceum? Would she be satisfied, I wonder, if I tell her it was the wand of the fairy that worked all sorts of magics? Certainly she would write back to me saying that I should buy that particular wand from the fairy and bring it home. Oh, I wish I could get that wand. How glad I would be if I could show my little daughter what Ray and Zack, the sweetest things ever I saw on the stage, had seen already, all those marvels and beauties of the Fairyland! Look at the gorgeous-coloured chrysanthemums, azaleas, poppies, bluebells, daffodils and many other flowers; and look again at what sort of people lived in this enchanting valley. Didn't a certain Miss Grannie Pickford dance gracefully? But Robert Roberty was altogether too strenuous for my Japanese taste. You can imagine how frightened I was, almost as frightened as Ray and Zack on the stage, seeing his whirlwind motion of running rather than dancing. It seems that I must modify my opinion of dancing since I came to London.

What changes of sceneries in this most innocent, most jolliest *Babes in the Wood*. I was highly pleased to be soon introduced to the happy village of Appledale, where all the inhabitants had to dress in picturesque fantasy and only dance and sing (wouldn't it be amusing to become one of them, and not worry about life's reality); and even Squire Snatch-all, I dare say, was rather delightful, although he declared at once: "Before I speak, allow me to say I am the vile villain of this play." Oh, what a wonderful declaration that is! Here comes Marmaduke, the Prodigal Son, who thought he might have been a squirrel as his father was a Squire and his mother a Squiress, returning from college (he never said what college), but he was quite clever to answer many questions in the scene of the schoolroom. He was asked, "Where is Germany?" He answered, "In England." And, besides, he said many more almost vulgar things. Is it not perfectly out of place, I thought, for this play of harmless amusement to have such a fun-making in conversation? It is a thing which should go to a variety house, for it hurts the other beauties of the pantomime (whatever meaning it may have) in its songs and stage-sceneries. I confess that I didn't expect from it such a bewilderment or medley of play, which reminded me of a Christmas pudding, rich in its own taste but rather difficult for a stranger to locate what it might be. I like Christmas pudding very well; though it might be a poor argument, I should say that for the same reason I like this play, which bears the name of pantomime only to make me understand.

Why! it has nothing about pantomime. It is a juvenile comic opera or a comic opera of ragtime merriment. (You have ragtime here in England, although that funny Marmaduke declared that he had it in America.) Again I say, "Can I eat Christmas pudding all the year round?" As I can only eat it once in a year, I should be greatly pleased to see the pantomime perhaps once a year; surely my head would grow dizzy when I had to see it too often. But how jolly it is to see it once a year at Christmas, and return for men to their days of boyhood and for boys to a thought of fairyland. It is never difficult to see why men as well as boys could enjoy this *Babes in the Wood*, but from a different point.

I would like to take my little son at home to see Stopum and Copum. I do not know which was the fatter. He would be tickled to death when he saw such a large policeman, who can even dance happily. Aren't Rob and Plunder, the bold robbers, wonderful to do this shameless work from receiving a few pence? It was the part most pleasing of the play that even the robbers could play some instrument and sing. But I was disappointed not finding a pantomime here.

On Boxing Day night (really I do not know what that means) I found myself at old Drury Lane, the "Home of Pantomimes," again not to find any pantomime there. In the *Sleeping Beauty* we had such a cunning little fairy boy called Puck, with horns on his head, which looked like those of a lobster. And, besides, there was a wicked fairy by the name of Anarchista using the most fairylike language. How beautifully Marcella, the Sleeping Beauty, sang when she finally awoke.

The play, or show, was perfectly marvellous, perhaps far more marvellous than *Babes in the Wood*, with those pretty girls in dancing or singing; I can hardly imagine how they had been trained. And what wonderful sceneries! It was the Duke of Monte Blanco that slept eighteen years; and I, the writer of this article, slept ten years, and am now awakened again in London at this Christmas time. And I am glad to be at this Drury Lane and taken by dear Puck to roam into Fairyland.

IV

"OH, WHAT A LOVELY COMPLEXION of these English women," I cannot help exclaiming. We have a Japanese proverb that the fair skin always hides seven blemishes in the face; how envious the Japanese women should be if they see the real English complexion—the most famous in all the world! And what a delightfully quick gait of the English women, what an eloquent charm! Oh! what a rhythm in it. And, above all, what a shape they have! My friend, an artist, who returned home after studying in England, always exclaimed: "It's perfectly hopeless to make anything good out of the Japanese women with such a poor shape awfully tortured from the habit of sitting and bowing. Look at the English women, whose straight forms look even proud, as if they have a personal responsibility for the universe! Oh, what a life in them! Perhaps you have seen an English actress in a Japanese play (are we Japanese thankful for it, or not? that is the question), imitating the Japanese woman particularly in her mincing gait. We cannot blame her, as our women walk as she imitates."

The other night I happened to talk with one clever Japanese lady here (I can assure you there are some clever women even among the Japanese), who said: "I was mistaken at first, suspecting that English women's conversation was made to hide their own thoughts. I often thought that they were fearing their secrets might be discovered. They had been trying, I thought, to mask themselves behind a screen; or perhaps famous fogs. As I said to you, it was my great mistake. When I became more acquainted with them, their frankness and sincerity became more clear to be seen. However, they are intellectual; I always feel that they are ever bent on improving my own poor mind." Then I asked her whether her mind had been improving. She smiled and declared that, whatever might happen, she should remain savage.

When I was here last I was told by a lady in her drawing-room that the English women were nothing but vanity, and I was assured by some fifty-fifth Duchess of Something that they were always martyrs to formality and etiquette. How are they now? I can remember clearly how

I was afraid (that is ten years ago) of this self-esteem and cool reserve; but my experiences of the last ten or fifteen days tell me that it was the exact case, quite reverse. I am having the time of my life, I confess, in talking with the English women at some receptions (however, I do not like the late hour for receptions), or by a supper table, where topics are delightfully light but without being vulgar; they are charmingly vivacious. And this epigrammatic turn of language and paradox? Why, if you blame it, you are certainly to blame Shaw and Chesterton. Yes, they are the teachers, are they not? The English women are wise and healthy; better still, they are quite simple. Such are the very points indeed I like in them.

I was mistaken when I thought that we are not supposed to expect anything interesting in first-class society. Although I cannot say I have seen it, I am glad to say (at least from what I have seen) that the English women carry their family history and a fat morocco-covered Bible quite lightly. And the most charming part with them is that, not only do they know how to talk, but also very well understand how to listen to the others, and besides, how to raise and drop their eyelashes. I often read in a book that it is the custom in English society for each to monopolise one woman, because she does not know how to be charming to a whole party. Now I think that such is a groundless accusation. In truth, what a delightful art the English women show in the reception-room; again, what a delightful art of theirs.

It is certainly a great treat to see them tastefully dressed. I often walk down the streets with one purpose, and that is to look at them. (I am sure they do not blame me for such a devotion.) But I confess that I had rather a poor opinion of them ten years ago; I even laughed and denounced their poor taste in dressing. I said then: "These English women hardly know how to raise their own skirts." They have nothing to do with their skirts now, since they wear such a light one which makes them look quite lovely, even coquettish. These ten years, it seems to me, taught them a great deal of dressing. And they have learnt well, I should like to say. I remember I had written, ten years ago, to my friend at home that the English women wore such ugly shoes (or boots, if you like), and their ankles might not have been charming enough to expose; but I should like to know now where is a woman whose shoes might be the subject to laugh at. Oh, what lovely shoes they wear now.

Not only in the matter of dressing, but their faces (of course, their shape and mane), had become much more attractive. To say they are as fresh as a daisy does them hardly any justice, since the daisy is more a flower of the countryside. I should like to compare them with chrysanthemums, which have recently been much beautified by horticulturists. The general culture improved their unsightly appearance. And what beautiful hair they have! It is said in Japan that woman's hair is always strong enough to pull an elephant. Where is a thing, I wonder, that an English woman cannot pull by her hair?

Although I never pretend to be a critic of women, I think I can say that I can see many more beautiful woman in five minutes in Bond Street than in any other place in the world.

V

I HAVE DURING MY PRESENT stay in England many incidents which, little as they are, shall not be forgotten. The following is one of them: As I had some important business to see a friend upon when I was in Oxford, I thought it proper to telegraph to him beforehand. I handed to the clerk of the neighbouring post-office a paper with writing to the effect that I should arrive at Puttington at half-past seven that night. Then I returned to my place and was busy making ready for my departure when the same clerk to whom I had given my message called on me with my telegraph paper to ask if I was not mistaken, as there was no train by which I would arrive at Puttington at half-past seven from Oxford. It most forcibly struck my Japanese mind that this act was the sweetest proof of English consideration, a thing that we never could even imagine in red-tape Japan. When I began truly to appreciate that heart of consideration, official or private, my reverence for great England at once increased a hundredfold. I took my hat off before this old European civilisation because of its own worthiness.

I confess, however, what mostly troubled my peace of mind was the matter of religion. I was tired presently with the hopeless aspect of the dirty Thames as would be any Japanese with, so to say, the heart of moon, flowers and wind. One day I went up the river to seek poetry in nature. And my object in straying into Putney was my faint desire to see Swinburne's old house as I once saw him somewhere in a picture, sitting in the grass of his back garden. It was my misfortune that I asked a clergyman to direct me to the right road, who began to talk on Christianity with such an earnestness, when I replied to him that I was a Buddhist. I was almost in danger of being converted on the spot, not because I was inspired by him, but because that seemed the only way to stop his speech. When we parted he held my hand firm and said: "We shall meet again in heaven."

When I was brought into Oxford, I found that the holy Cross was staring on my heathen soul with great pity from those twenty and odd college buildings. The solemnity of thirty and more churches practically jammed in such a small place as only the districts of Ushigome and Koishikawa of Tokyo combined, chilled my Oriental heart, and made me think it difficult to associate with Christianity. I did not take many days before I discovered what power the priests had, publicly or privately, in England. While many exceptions should be allowed in this matter of religion as any other thing, one can say quite safely that the English religious belief is still unshaken. Let the non-believers declare whatever they wish. The general conservatism of English faith has much to do with forming the manly part of England's civilisation.

Once I was a guest of a well-known scholar whose youngest boy of years always put the house in an uproar by his raging. He was ready to fight with his elder sister, holding up a pen-holder, when I entered the parlour. The mother suddenly appeared to rescue the girl, and scolded the boy, who cried loudly, saying that she was wrong, not he. The mother smiled, and asked him, with a few gentle taps on his head, if he was a Christian. When he said he was, she put a further question if he knew well what was next to "Give us our daily bread" in the Lord's Prayer. The boy made a guilty face at once, and threw away the pen-holder as his childish soul wished to repent. I thought, then, it was the most beautiful picture ever I had seen since I came into England. It is too heavy a question whether it is the happiest way to bring up children, but I have little hesitation to affirm there is more good than harm in it.

I can say I saw first in my life what the "home" really means in England, since it has yet in Japan to be cultivated more conscientiously. I observed clearly that the best effort was given for its development. My own experience with the English home was of the sweetest kind; the open-heartedness and simplicity which are the best entertainment prevail in verily satisfactory fashion. Even the way of spreading round the things artistic or otherwise, which bewildered my Japanese sense of art, more glad to use the "poetry of concealment" to advantage, soon began to encourage my psychological turn of mind for the better understanding of the English temperament. The seeming childishness is decidedly a strength, while the Japanese art of humility in hiding proves more often to be hypocritic. I cannot help laughing over the little comedies I enacted in spite of myself, when I could not wholly forget that the Japanese way of etiquette is not to emphasize one's likes, or more important to observe, to speak but moderately of the things you dislike. Once I was brought into an uncomfortable situation when I let a word of enthusiasm slip over a cheese before me, in truth, without much thought, and I was obliged to look jolly with various kinds of cheese which appeared taking my word for a pledge. It was truly a good dose to cure the weakness of Oriental etiquette which is at best only foolishness. I make it my custom to warn myself not to demonstrate my Japanese way of politeness, which always turns out wrong. The Japanese mind, like any other Japanese thing, only works upside down to that of Englishmen.

I am not ready to discuss the respective merits of English and German people on the subject of musical taste; but I will say that the popularisation of music is more thorough in England than in Germany. I have had such a difficulty to excuse myself from being well cornered into singing a song or two. I often wonder if there is another people like the Japanese, especially the Japanese of the younger generation, whose lack of musical culture is appalling. I could not make myself so obliging as my friend M——, who always sang the National Anthem whenever he was asked for a Japanese song. I have only to say that I could not help admiring his courage in singing it. I agree with all the English people that music is most necessary to make the "evening" successful. I have often thought that they are almost scientific in making it happy. And how obliging they are to one another for that purpose! I had a few occasions, like any other Japanese, when I acted even admirably a big feature of the "evening." The comical side of the affair that even I myself pretended to be something wonderful under the circumstances cannot be forgotten all my life. What jolly harmless English people!

The other day I read in a Japanese magazine a humorous article written by M. O., how he, with his friend, played a most difficult rôle as "Japanese experts" of the Go game at the Hastings and St. Leonards Chess Club. (So he too!) I wish to see his uncomfortable face when his picture was printed, of course, as the famous Go player, in the Hastings newspaper. I sympathise with him when he tried his utmost to look serious, while he was playing a "game of conspiracy" with his friend before the people. I think I have no right whatever to tell his secret to English readers.

I take much interest in all questions, political as well as social; my Orientalism did not interfere with my enthusiasm over the Woman Suffragists. I rarely missed reading in the papers the witty saying or clever repartee which overflows from the debates in the Houses and the speeches on the platform, and many of them are stamped deeply on my mind. I could not imagine before that the English freedom of speech had such a full meaning; it is clear that it was an evidence of English fearlessness in facing the problems of humanity and justice. If the English people are loyal toward their king, that is not because he happens to sit upon the throne, but because he is a powerful defender of righteousness and the people.

And again I will say that if they love their own country it is only from their unshakeable belief that she is the first country of the world. I frequently thought it was rather silly for them to put that eternally same "first in the world" in this and that. Is it not, I wonder, the most dangerous superstition of all superstitions? While I admit that their belief in "first in the world" has greatly helped to make the country really the first in the world, as in fact she is, I think, on the other hand, there is a danger for them in denying any merit to another country. Not only once, but quite often, I was asked even by an educated person if we had electricity and railroads in Japan. We have, I think, to blame the English authors of books on Japan, whose delight and admiration are only in the things of old Japan.

I have no slightest hesitation to declare that I had my greatest days at Oxford. It was perfectly delightful to see there what a sweet old-fashioned love existed between the teachers and students. The fact reminded me of our old feudal times, when Bushido and Confucian ethics governed the country in the most respectable way. I am no person fit for writing of the physical civilisation of the English people; beside, I have only a little interest when I compare it with the other side of humanity. Dear old England with mother-love and consideration! It is her humanity that makes her great in the world.

VII

Kicho No Ki

Home, 8*th October* 1904

Japan again!—*kicho* after eleven years! I left New York in August; and it was the 6th of October when I left Shinbashi, Tokyo, homeward bound.

I stopped at Fujizawa, where my priest brother has the Jokoji temple; with him, I started to see Enoshima—that enchanted isle of Benten Sama. It reminded me of a certain Hy-Brasail of Irish song; oh, is it not an angel's home rising sudden out of a sacred water? Then we went to see Daibutsu or the Great Buddha of Kamakura; how I wished it stood by the seashore! Why? Daibutsu's mighty profundity in silence and thought discarding the voice of the sea would show more sublime.

Under the soft greyness of evening we came back to the temple; and I stopped over night in the Buddhistic quietness which bit my soul; it was the first experience of my life. I know that I felt it more than I ought as I was fresh from the noisy American life. Next morning I was startled from my sleep by "*Gan, gan, gan!*" the sound of a bell; it told me that my priest brother was beginning his morning prayer.

I took the six o'clock train toward Nagoya. I felt a great disappointment not hearing the "swan-like rhapsody of dying night" in Fujisan's lotos-peak soaring through the morning ether. However, I was in a measure comforted later at Suzukawa, when he peeped out from the clouds upon me. There was no word to express his majesty and grace. I felt as if I were happily running through a dreamlike garden; it would not be too much to say that no other train in the world harvests so much natural beauty with its wheels as this Tokaido's.

I was grateful for the "preservation of a recall of primeval Nature," the "exemption of the soil from labour" in Chinju no Mori, a village shrine; as it has been said, nothing but "long ages, respectful care, sometimes fortunate neglect," could make such an ideal wilderness. Since it is in the war time, I saw many a Rising Sun flag among the green trees, beyond the yellow rice fields; my patriotism jumped high with the sight of the flag. I felt in my heart to shout *Banzai*. The water ran clear, the birds flew up and down. I thought there could be no other country like Japan so beautiful. I reached Tsushima, my native town, at evening.

I frightened my old father at the station, who was actually trying to find me among some other people. There is no wonder that he could not recognise me; I must have changed a great deal. "We must make a thanking worship immediately to Tenno Sama; I have been praying for his protection for you all the time. It is, of course, through his divine favour we have you here making a safe return," he exclaimed.

My mother was crying before she spoke. I wept too.

"How glad you came home! I was afraid we might not see you any more. And how you have changed, Yone Ko! You almost look like a *Seiyojin*, your nose and eyes just like those of a Western-sea man. Oh, how glad—you have returned finally!"

And she cried again.

My arrival was reported speedily among the people of Nakajima Cho, my street; the old men and women from the neighbouring houses, and the friends of my boyhood days, who were now the fathers of many children, began to call on me. They couldn't raise their heads from reverence and fear before me; what gentle souls. I could not help crying secretly when Oito San, the old lady neighbour, said that Okuwa Sama—my mother's name—used to say she wished to die after having seen me once again.

How sweet is home!

I tasted the best thing ever I had in my life in a simple dinner which my mother prepared.

The president of the Tsushima Grammar School called on me at night, and wished me to make a speech before his students. The younger people of my street were all for giving a dinner in my honour. All the guests left my house at about ten o'clock. Before I went to bed, I was calmly rubbed by a shampooer.

I went to sleep to the lullaby of pine trees which the gentle winds sent to me; I knew it came from Kojoji, my neighbouring temple, and it was a familiar sound too.

HOME, 10*th*

I was no other than Rip Van Winkle, only not so romantic as Joseph Jefferson's. I could not recognise even my elder brother who was waiting to receive me at the Yokohama station; and I will say too that the glance he cast upon me was perfectly indifferent. We got in the same train toward Tokyo; at Shinbashi I found out that he was my brother Fujitaro, when he joined with a party in which I recognised at once Madame Isonaga, the lady who used to look after me with motherly care; the party was meant for my honour.

There is no wonder at all if I did not recognise even one person in my neighbouring houses, as I had not been home for over seventeen years. It was O Maki San, really—my neighbour's girl, who used to dress her hair in girlish *mitsuwa* or "three rings" in the dear old days—now the mother of three children. Who was that young man who said, "It's a long time now, Yone Sama—?" Why, he was Kii San, the son of the carpenter Hanroku San. He was only six or seven years old, when I was in my tenth or eleventh year; I used to take him with me to Rodo San's to be taught penmanship. He is not a boy now, but the proud father of two children. "Do you remember this picture of Daikoku Sama (God of Luck) you drew for me such a long time ago?"—thus I was addressed by one person; and he was Hikobey San's Hiko San, the child I loved best. I used to give him my pictures of orchid or chrysanthemum; and I remember now that I was once scolded by my mother when I showed her a large piece of *shuzumi* or red ink which he gave me by way of acknowledgment of my pictures. "You mustn't receive anything from such a little child," my mother said; I remember it as if it were only yesterday. "You grew pretty large," I said. "Yes, I married last spring," he answered.

I am told that two young men of our street are at the front; and one of them has been wounded already, and now he is in the Nagoya hospital; and the other is the adopted son of the neighbour on the left hand. Although his mother-in-law patriotically submitted, saying, "It is for our country's sake," I could clearly espy her voiceless complaint; her daughter, the wife of her soldier son, is sick in bed while her two children cry. Ojto San is a diligent person as my mother says; as I hear, she is working since morning on her loom for a new *kimono;* and I am sure it may be meant for her son on his safe return.

A while ago my father brought me an official announcement to read for him; it was to bid us make our presence to see the soldiers off to the front. Let us give them words of glory; they may be killed or wounded, if lucky.

Last night we all lighted our front gate lanterns to express our joy over the Lio Yang victory. We do not make any noise even in joy; and are facing the war with such a silence which is only the voice of life and death.

Kami Sama or the gods do not undergo any worldly change of fortune; but at a time like this their glory reaches high water mark. It goes without saying that to say Kami Sama here at Tsushima means Gozu Tenno. The big wood fires will be burned right before the shrine all night; the daily worshippers, doubtless the relations of soldiers at the front, are said to be more than five hundred. A few *sen* will make you the happy possessor of an *omamori* or charm which will very likely protect your fighters from bad luck; and a special prayer will be given to you on your appeal.

This Tsushima is a slight town snugly lying as if on the bottom of a basin; but her dream has been stirred considerably by the establishment of a railroad station where the strange people from another part of the country flow out as if through a break in a dyke. The Middle School added a new dignity to the town; and the Tsushima Grammar School is said to be the model in this Aichi province. That school I can see from my upstairs window; and I have been looking with a strange feeling of interest over the rows of little girls' heads now for some while. Listen, what are they singing? Even the girls must sing the war songs nowadays. What lovely voices! I felt glad to think that they did not loose their girlish beauty of voice in such a thrilling stir.

I can see also through the upstairs shoji one big pine tree of Kojoji wherein, it is said, many a *hitodama* or human soul looking like a ladle with lantern-like light went floating in just before the day of death; it is the very tree, where, as my mother observed, my sister's *hitodama* disappeared one or two evenings before her final sleep.

Poor little Tsune who died in her ninth year! I have to beg her forgiveness for many things. I was a terrible boy, full of mad mischief, I believe.

KYOTO, 28*th*

To see the beauty of a Japanese autumn, it is said, you must come to Kyoto; and I was just in time, to my joy. The evening light is certainly sweet in autumn with longer night; and I am pleased to be in Kyoto with *andon* and candle-sticks; they are the sweetest of lights.

Here I feel as if I had flown back to the sixteenth century—the dear age of slow life, half song and half sorrow; what a contrast to Tokyo, to America! We are trying hard to hide our weariness of the modern civilisation; but one cannot help exclaiming in delight over such a perfectly undisturbed oasis as Kyoto, where you can sing the oldest song, and let the world go by as it pleases. Our modern Japan is going mad over every sort of Western thing; but Kyoto is singing alone the song of protest.

"How stout you did grow," I said to Mr. Taki, the son of a rich Nagoyo merchant, who is managing his father's business at Kyoto. He was one of my best friends in my middle school days; he was awaiting me at the station. "I knew at once it was you by your sharp eyes," he said.

I wanted for some time to see the gracefully gracious shape of Higashi Yama, which, as some well-known poet wrote, looks a sleeping beauty under a *futon* or quilt. I decided at once that I must take a walk this evening at least as far as to get a sight of the mountain. When I was startled by the sudden music of water—why, is this Kamo Gawa? The sleeping mountain was right before me. You impolite thing, it's not the Japanese way at all to receive a guest lying like that. But I will excuse you. The moon rose. I thought it quite lucky to see, as I stood on the bridge over Kamo Gawa, the same moon which was sung and sung by the thousand *uta* poets, those nobles and princesses of Japan's golden age—it is a long time ago now.

Next day, I with Mr. Taki started to Arashi Yama to see the beauty of autumn; and I found it there in splendour. What a wonder—the most rare sight of the mountain and river through the tinted mists of *momiji* or maple leaves, the mists now floating an ear, as if addressing us, now sailing afar as if singing the sad song of farewell. I felt I saw a certain *tennin* or angel in the leaves, which, to disappoint me, turned at once to a cloud moving terribly; it might be that the heart-burned leaves exchanged speech with the passing wind.

We engaged three men, presently, to push the boat up the valley; the water was so rapid that they were obliged to pull it by a rope; and it often stopped to bite the rock like a dog. We turned the head of our boat back at Hotsugawa, where we invited three mountain girls to ride down with us; they were doubtless going to Kyoto to sell the dry brushwood which they carried; they are an *owarame* whose rustic yet poetical simplicity is known over Japan. The youngest and prettiest of them began busily to arrange her hair by the looking-glass of the water, soon after we started; I thought she wanted to look her very best as she would soon reach Kyoto, or it might not be impossible that her lover was awaiting her, perhaps at Kotokiki Bashi. About this bridge I should like to explain briefly. It was just here, it is believed, that Nakakuni, the imperial messenger to the Lady Kogo, the beloved mistress of the Emperor Takakura no. In—she had hidden herself from the jealousy of Taira no Kiyomori, the father of the Empress—the story is quite an old one—heard the Lady Kogo's playing of *koto* music at last. Indeed he had sought her there one moon night in the very thought that she would play it longing after the sweet days of the past. Hence this name Kotokiki Bashi, the *Koto-Hearken* bridge. It would be idle to ask about the truth of such a thing; but it is sure that she—poor Lady Kogo—hid herself under the *momiji* of Saga's deeper hills, where you might say with Sarumaru Dayu:

> "How sad is autumn,—
> When you hear the deer's cry,
> With his hoofs upon the maple leaves,
> Amid the deeper hill!

We dined this night at Hyotei, the unique tea-house in the silent ground of the Nanzenji temple. When we left the house, plenty of stars shone, and the moon was soon expected. The purple light of a Kyoto star is the purple colour you will find in Kyoto's *yuzenzome*—design of girl's clothes; oh, what beauty! The girl of the restaurant gave us a little lantern with the roughly drawn picture of a gourd (by the way, Hyotei means the "Gourd House") to light the darkness of night. On the way to Mr. Taki's house I felt I heard a sad music of the stars—perhaps the *koto* music of the Lady Kogo.

I couldn't help thinking of her.

NARA, *2nd November*

Now I am in a far older city than Kyoto; Nara, the capital of the eighth century, with its avenues of lichen-patched stone lanterns, and with a hundred temple bells echoing down the calm groves, an Olympus of *uta* poem and art in those lyric ages of Japan. I smelled at once the classical odour of *uta* which is, however, not more than a sigh; I wondered why I did not bring with me the *Manyoshu* (the first and most esteemed anthology of verse of that century), or any *uta* book at least. And I was making my presence in a *yofuku* or foreign dress—such a modern informal sack coat!—I thought that *eboshi* and *shitatare* which were worn by the courtiers in those days were the proper outfit for such an old city of incense and dream. I sought any book of *uta* at a bookshop on Sanjo; instead, I found a worn copy of FitzGerald's *Rubáiyát* of Omar. But I thought that the dear old man would not find this place entirely uncongenial; surely he could make a paradise with the help of a lady and *saké* out of this tired city.

There is no more pleasing sight than those deer with the peaceful eyes; they must be the same peaceful eyes as those of the deer who, it is said, brought the god Kasuga Myojin here. I was perfectly happy that they did not look at me with any scornful look. I fed them with *senbes* which I bought from a girl who was selling them for this purpose. I walked under the cedars and pines, now having the deer before me, now after me; I even ventured to imagine that I might be a Kasuga Myojin. Indeed, I thought that here the silent spirit of a god is visible as a mist, and it was not impossible to grasp it by the hand. I always believed that the colour of silence should be green, while red is the colour of faith; here I saw the red-painted shrine amid the green leaves.

The three little girls danced for me a *shinto* dance; I was given by the official attendant of the shrine a slip of paper with the name of the god written on it, and a little bit of rice wrapped in a paper. They were such a trifling thing; but I did not dare to throw them on the roadside. If I did, I was afraid some evil would hold me up.

I bought a few combs and hairpins made out of the horns of the deer, as souvenirs. I will tell you that nobody—not even the souvenir-sellers—will tell any story on this holy ground.

Daibutsu or the Great Buddha of Nara was far bigger than that at Kamakura; I could not understand how the Japanese who made such an immense idol in the old days came to be considered clever only with small things. The Buddhism which teaches you a big religion must have a big thing materially, I fancy.

A few *sen* gave me a right to strike Daibutsu's bell hanging at the tower; I struck it. "*Boon, boon, boon!*" What sorrow and profundity in the sound! The voice of the bell is the voice of Buddhism; it echoes adown heaven and earth. I bent my head, and prayed. *Nam amida butsu, nam amida butsu!*

The autumn sun was quickly sinking when I finished the Tofukuji temple, and general Nara *Kenbutsu*. I confess that the Mikasa hill so famous in the ancient *uta* was a disappointment. However, shall I wait to see the moon on it?

Now the Daibutsu bell tolled evening; the birds returned to their nest; the air of Nara entered into solemnity from peace. I was slightly thrilled, and looked back at the *goju no to* or pagoda on whose top one star appeared.

"*Boon, boon, boon!*"

There are a few moments, at least, when we have a free breathing space before our final end; it was our foolishness, I remember well, to think that Tsune would live when she calmly began to talk something, which was, alas, her good-bye. And so it is with the year, which will not go without showing her last beauty before her winter's sleep; and that means the maple leaves, of course. The *momiji* in our garden, which were planted by grandfather, are pretty near the last day of their glory; some leaves are already on the ground. Ye maples, voiceless singers of the Japanese autumn, your song is the song of heart and blood. I always suspect the sincerity of the cherry blossom whose gaiety is altogether extraordinary. I am with ye, *momiji* and autumn; ye are the soul of the Japanese poet which is sad. Sadness is a blessing.

I wished before I made *kicho* I could raise chrysanthemums to my heart's content, staying at my home; but it seems now that it is far too much to wish. And so it may be for many years more. "You might arrange this flower in the vase, Yone," my mother said, and brought a few chrysanthemums from the garden yard. I received a lesson or two in the way of flower arrangement; but I am now awfully degenerated. The flowers would, if I touched them, be frightened by the toughness of my fingers.

"Oh, cold, *obarsama!* Give me a padded *kimono;* the snows are falling on Tado mountain," little Yoshi saying, returned from her school. She is my eldest brother's girl who is growing under the particular care of her grandmother. Indeed, the autumn will soon be done; since morning I heard the wind singing on the pine tree of Kojoji; it seemed to be tuning for the winter song. The voice of a bird was cold too. For the last eleven years I have been spending myself without any special attention to spring and autumn; in fact, the American cities drove Nature out. But here in Japan, especially at home, I am again with Nature—dear old thing!—I can count every breath of her's; her each step echoes distinctly on my mind. It is very difficult, I dare say, not to become a poet in Japan.

I attended the welcome dinner given to me by the whole town of Tsushima at evening; there were more than two hundred people, among them the mayor of the town and the member of the House of

Commons whom the town elected. When I returned home from the dinner, I found that my mother was warming my night robe over the fire-box. Dear mother!

It was my father's voice that I overheard as he lay in bed: "It's now one month since Yone returned home. Really the time seems short when it's gone; we have been waiting for eleven years, thinking that he would come home today or tomorrow." "Yes, oh yes! He will leave us, he says, on the day after tomorrow; I think that I will make an *ohagi* (a sort of pudding) for him. I remember he used to like it very well," my mother said. Then I heard again both of them rejoicing that we—the three other brothers and I—had turned out mighty good as men. "There's no greater thing to be proud of for the family," they said.

A moment later, my mother called loudly from beyond the screen: "Shall I give you one more quilt, Yone Ko? The night is cold."

I had so many callers next day as my departure was told among the people. Many of them brought me many letters to be delivered to their sons in San Francisco or in Chicago; doubtless they thought that America is just as small as Japan, where you can go in a day or two from one place to another. And some of them brought a little boy aged seven or eight hoping I might take him with me to "wonderful Amerikey!" They presented me one thing or another to bid me farewell. Dear simple country souls!

My father made ready for me plenty of hot water for the bath tub; my niece came to me and said: "*Obarsuma* said, Uncle, you shall wash yourself well as this is the last night at home." "Yoshi, tell her that I will save some dirt to come home again and wash it," I replied.

My mother was busy making my *kimono* ready in this night.

I am starting for Tokyo tomorrow morning wearing a kimono and wooden clogs as a Japanese does. I missed them for such a long time.

But they are with me again.

VIII

Isamu's Arrival in Japan

The arrival of my two-year-old boy, Isamu, from America was anticipated, as it is said here, with crane-neck-long longing. This Mr. Courageous landed in Yokohama on a certain Sunday afternoon of early March, when the calm sunlight, extraordinarily yellow, as it happens to be sometimes, gave a shower bath to the little handful of a body half-sleeping in his "nurse carriage," as we call it here—and, doubtless, half-wondering, with a baby's first impression of Japan, many-coloured and ghostly. Now and then he opened a pair of large brown eyes. "See papa;" Léonie tried to make Isamu's face turn to me; however, he shut his eyes immediately without looking at me, as if he were born with no thought of a father. In fact, he was born to my wife in California some time after I left America. Mrs. N—— attempted to save me from a sort of mortification by telling me how he used to sing and clap his hands for "papa to come" every evening.

I thought, however, that I could not blame him after all for his indifference to father, as I did not feel, I confess, any fatherly feeling till, half an hour ago, I heard his crying voice for the first time by the cabin door of the steamer *Mongolia* before I stepped in; I was nobody yet, but a stranger to him. He must have, to be sure, some time to get acquainted with me, I thought; and how wonderful a thing was a baby's cry! It is true that I almost cried when I heard Isamu's first cry. I and my wife slowly pushed his carriage toward the station, I looking down to his face, and she talking at random. Isamu appeared perfectly brown as any other Japanese child; and that was satisfactory. Mrs. N—— said that he was brown all over when he was born; however, his physical perfection was always a subject of admiration among the doctors of her acquaintance. I felt in my heart a secret pride in being his father; but a moment later, I was really despising myself, thinking that I had no right whatever to claim him, when I did not pay any attention to him at all for the last three years. "Man is selfish," I said in my heart; and again I despised myself.

I learned that he made the whole journey from Los Angeles sitting like a prince on the throne of his little carriage; he even went to sleep in it on the steamer. He was ready to cry out whenever he lost sight of it; it was the dearest thing to him, second only to the bottle of milk, for which he invented the word "Boo." We thought that it would be perfectly easy to take the carriage with us on board the train, as we could fold it up; but the conductor objected to our doing so, as it belonged to the category of "breakables." And we had to exclaim, "Land of red tape, again," at such an unexpected turn. Isamu cried aloud for "Baby's carriage" when the train reached the Shinbashi station of Tokyo; we put him again in his carriage, and pushed it by Ginza, the main street. And there my wife and baby had their first supper in Japan; Baby could hardly finish one glass of milk.

It was after eight in the evening when we took the outer-moat car line toward my house in Hisakata Machi—quite poetical is this Far-beyond Street, at least in name—wrapping Baby's carriage in a large *furoshiki*. It may have been from his kindness that the conductor did not raise objection. But afterward, when we had to change cars at Iidabashi Bridge, we met again a flat denial to our bringing it in; and we had to push it about a mile more of somewhat hilly road under the darkness. A few stars in the high sky could not send their light to the earth; the road was pretty bad as it was soon after the snow, though our Tokyo streets are hardly better at any other time. And it was rather a cold night. It goes without saying that my wife must have been tired of nursing Isamu all through the voyage; he had been sea-sick, and had eaten almost nothing. Where was the fat baby which she used to speak of in her letters? It was sad, indeed, to see Isamu, pale and thin, wrapped in a blanket, keeping quiet in his carriage; and now and then he opened his big eyes, and silently questioned the nature of the crowd which, though it was dark, gathered round us here and there. His little soul must have been wondering whither he was being taken. And we must have appeared to people's eyes quite unusual. In no more than the dying voice of an autumn insect, Baby suddenly asked mother where was his home. I am sure that not only Isamu, but tired Léonie, too, wished to know where it was.

I think that it was not altogether unreasonable for Baby to keep crying all the time; I was rather suspicious, looking at Léonie, that her heart also wanted a heartful cry from the heavy, exotic oppression, whose novelty had passed some time ago. "*Karan, koron, karan, koron*"—the high-pitched song which was strung out endlessly from the Japanese wooden clogs on the pavement, especially in the station, had that forlorn kind of melody whose monotony makes you sad; and I daresay Isamu thought that the Japanese speech might be a devil's speech—in fact, it is, as one of the earliest Dutch missionaries proclaimed. I noticed he raised his ears whenever he heard it. (By the way, he has already come to handling this devil's speech. My writing was interrupted awhile ago by his persistent request—in Japanese—to be taken to see his Japanese aunt; he is quite happy here as he can have as many aunts as he wishes.) And still he did not stop crying even after his safe arrival at this Hisakata home; it tried my patience very much, and I did not know really what to do with him. He cried on seeing the new faces of the Japanese servant girls, and cried more when he was spoken to by them. I got a few Japanese toys ready for him, a cotton-made puppy among them, as I was told a dog was his favourite; but he could not think that they were meant to amuse and not to hurt him, and the dog did not appear to him like a dog at all, but as something ugly. And he cried terribly. "*Okashi*," one of the servants, brought a piece of Japanese cake, thinking it would surely stop his cry. But he cried the more, exclaiming, "No, no!" The cake did not look to him like a cake.

The night advanced; a blind shampooer passed before the house, playing a bamboo flute. Isamu, though he was doubtless sleepy, caught its music, and jumped out of his little bed, exclaiming: "Andrew, mama!" A man by the name of Andrew Anderson, Léonie explained, used to call at his California home almost every evening, and sing to them in a sweet, high Swedish voice; so that his little memories were returning to him. For the last month, since the day of his departure from Los Angeles, his poor head had been whirring terribly through nightmare spectacles. Poor Isamu! But I felt happy in thinking that he was just beginning to feel at home even in Japan.

"Baby, where are you going?" I asked him, when he was making his way toward the front door; he stood still by the door, and caught another note of the shampooer's flute, and again cried most happily: "Oh, Andrew, Andrew!" However, he was sad a few moments later, not seeing any Andrew come in; and he began to cry. But sleepiness overtook him immediately; and I found him soon sleeping soundly in his own bed.

When two or three days had passed, he stopped crying, although he was yet far from being acquainted with his Japanese home. I found him trying to find something in the house which might interest his little mind. There are many *shojis*, or paper sliding-doors, facing the garden;

they have a large piece of glass fixed up in their centres, over which two miniature *shojis* open and shut from right and left; and they caught his interest. He had been busy, I was told one day, opening and shutting them again since the morning; when I saw him doing it, he was just exclaiming: "Mama, see boat!" It was his imagination, I think, that he caught sight of a certain ship; he was still thinking that he was sailing over the ocean on the steamer. Surely it was that. When he stepped into the house, I observed that he was quite cautious about tumbling down; it was very funny to see his way of walking.

On the fifth day, he earnestly begged his mother to go home. "Where's Nanna!" he asked her. His grandmother, Mrs. Gilmour, who still remains in Los Angeles, was called by Isamu, "Nanna;" he began to recall her to his memory, and to miss her a great deal, as she was the dearest one next to his mother. When Léonie answered him "Far far," in the baby's speech, he repeated it several times to make himself understand; and he turned pale and silent at once. He was sad. "Baby, go and see papa," my wife said to him; he slowly stole toward my room, and slightly opened my *shoji*, when I looked back. He banged it at once, and ran away crying: "No, no!" I overheard him, a moment later, saying to Léonie that I was not there. I must have appeared to his eye as some curiosity, to look at once in a while, but never to come close to. However, I was not hopeless; and I thought that I must win him over, and then he would look at me as he did his mother.

Isamu noticed that I clapped my hands to call my servant girls, and they would answer my clapping with "*Hai!*"—that is the way of a Japanese house. And he thought to himself, of course to my delight, that it was proper for him to answer "*Hai*" to my handclapping, and he began to run toward me before the girls, and kneel before me as they did, and wait for my words. I was much pleased to see that he was growing familiar with me. And he even attempted to call me "Danna Sama" (Mr. Lord), catching the word which the servants respectfully addressed to me. It was too much, I thought; however, I could not help smiling delightedly at it. My wife could not take to Japanese food at once; but I found that Baby was perfectly at home with it. I discovered, when he quietly disappeared after our breakfast, that he was enjoying his second Japanese meal with the servants. When they objected to him one morning, I overheard him exclaiming: "*Gohan, gohan*" (honourable rice). His love of Japanese rice was really remarkable.

Every morning, when an *ameya*, or wheat gluten seller, the delight of Japanese children, passed by the house beating his drum musically, Isamu's heart would jump high, and he would dance wildly, exclaiming: "*Donko, don, donko, don, don,*" and get on the back of a servant—any back he could find quickest—to be carried like a Japanese child. This *ameya* is, indeed, a wonderful man for children: for one *sen* or so he will make a miniature fox, dog, *tengu*, or anything imaginable with wheat gluten.

At first he was not pleased to ride on the girl's back; but soon it became an indispensable mode of carriage for him. It is ready for him any time; and the Japanese girl's large *obi* tied on her somewhat bended back makes a comfortable seat. And the funniest part is that Isamu thinks that the girl's back is called "*Donko, don, donko, don.*" As our servants did not know a word of English, they could not express their invitation to get on their backs; and it happened, when an *ameya* passed by, that one of them acted as if he were being carried on her back, repeating the sound of the *ameya's* drum: "*Donko, don, donko, don.*" Isamu caught the meaning on the spot, and jumped on her back. And afterward, this "*Donko, don, donko, don,*" became a most useful word. When the girls say it, showing their backs, he thinks it proper, and even courteous, for him to get on them; and he will hunt a girl, repeating it, when he wishes to go out pick-a-back. And, again, its usefulness grew still more a day or two ago; he started to use it even when he wished only to go for a walk. I heard him saying to Léonie: "Oh, mamma, *donko, don, donko, don!*"

He showed a certain pride in learning a few Japanese words which could be understood by the people around him. And he made it his business to sit down like a Japanese and say "*Sayonara*" when a guest leaves the house; and he likes doing it. He shouted "*Banzai*" for the first time the day my brother brought him two paper flags, one of them being, of course, Japanese, while the other was an American one. "You Japanese baby?" Léonie asked him. "Yes," he replied, turning to me. And when I asked him how he would like to remain an American, he would turn to my wife and say: "Yes." He was the cause of no small sensation among the Japanese children of this Koishikawa district, at least; his foreign manner and Western tint, and also the point of his having a Japanese father, I should say, made him a wonderful thing to look at for the children around here, while they felt some kinship with him. The fame of Isamu spread over many miles; even a *jinrikisha* man far away will tell you where "Baby San" lives, although N——'s name may mean nothing to his ear. The children think, I am sure, that "Baby" is his own name; and whenever they pass by our house, morning or evening, they will shout loudly: "Baby San." And Isamu will rarely miss a chance to run out and show himself in answer. The little fellow is quite vain already. And the children who caught the word of "Mama" spoken by Isamu to his mother, thought that it was Léonie's name. I am told by her that she was frequently startled by a shout of "Mama San" from behind in the street. To be the mother of "Baby San" is not at all bad. I felt happy to see that he began to play with the Japanese children. We have a little play called "Mekakushi;" many children will make a large ring with joined hands, and choose a child and let him stand in the middle of the rings with his eyes covered with his palms. Mekakushi means "eyes hidden." The child at the centre will walk to the ring, and touch any child, and tell its right name; and then the child who was told its own name will take its turn to be in the middle. It happened one evening that our Isamu was obliged to stand in the centre; his bewilderment was clear, for he never knew the children's real names. But accidentally, Léonie passed by on her way home; he took advantage of the chance at once, and called out loudly: "Mama, mama!" I am not told whether my wife fulfilled her duty to stand in the middle or not, however; we talked about it afterwards, and laughed.

Our large, oval, wooden Japanese bath-tub furnishes him with one of the most pleasing of objects. He will get in it even when the water is hardly warm; he does not mind cold water a bit. If I happen to see him in there, he will proudly let me admire his stomach, which is, in fact, big for such a little child; it is his proudest exhibit. He calls it "Baby's Bread-basket;" I cannot help smiling when I think that it was wisely named. We have a little folklore story of a monkey and a tortoise; the latter was outwitted by the former when he attempted to get the monkey's liver. Mrs. N—— told him of this story, changing the liver to stomach; the variation was effective, and took his little heart by storm. A day or two later, when a monkey player dropped into our house, and made the monkey dance, he kept watching its stomach; and when it was gone, he was tremendously sorry that he could not get near enough to see it.

Isamu hates anything which does not move, or makes no noise. When he has nothing new to play with, he will begin to open and shut the *shojis;* when he tires of that, he will try to go around the house and hunt after the clocks which I hid, as they lost the right track of the time since he came. And presently I send him away with a servant to the Botanical Garden to look at and feed the "kwakwa," as he calls the ducks.

He made a habit of playing with our shadows on the walls of the sitting-room after supper every evening. "Mama, shadow gone! Give Baby shadow, mama," he will exclaim, sulkily seeing his own shadow disappear. "Go to papa! He will give it to you," Léonie will say; then he will hunt for it, pushing his hand everywhere about my dress. "There it is, Baby," I will say, seeing his shadow accidentally appear on the wall. How delighted he is! He is not pleased to go to bed if he does not see the moon. But I doubt if he has any real knowledge of the moon. When I say that he must go to bed, he will go outside the door, and say there is no moon yet. Then I quietly steal into the drawing-room and light a large hanging lamp with a blue-coloured globe, and say to him: "Moon is come now. See it, Baby!" He will be mighty pleased with it; a few minutes later, he will be in bed, soundly sleeping. Really, his sleeping face looks like a miniature Buddha idol, as Léonie wrote me long ago.

Any child appears wonderful to his father; so is Isamu to me. I confess that I made many new discoveries of life and beauty since the day of his arrival in Japan. I never pass by a store in the street without looking at the things which might belong to children.

IX

The Story of my Own Uncle

I awoke to the song of the nightingale. (Such a beginning may sound, I am afraid, prosaic in these days of disillusion.) Negishi of my recent residence, however, is one of the few places in Tokyo still with old reminiscences clinging gossamer-like, where the nightingale always associated with ancient art does not look out of place. My attention, which had become my morning habit while stretching forth my body in bed, was interrupted at once most harshly by the bells of a newsboy; I knew that the *Tokyo Asahi* was already in my mail-box. When I called the housegirl for the paper, the nightingale, certainly indignant at the discord of modern life, gracefully slipped away. The shaft of the sun pierced through the pane into my room.

I opened the paper mechanically, without any desire for news, my body still attached to the pillow; my eyes were suddenly drawn to the picture of an old woman, no one but the mother of Denjiro Kotoku, the so-called anarchist, who had been condemned to the gallows; it was an announcement of her death. I am told that she stood, a week or ten days ago, before her son's cell, to say her farewell after making a long, tiresome journey to Tokyo from far-away Tosa, this old lady of seventy years, and advised Kotoku: "Make your last moment manlike! You must never act like a coward." She died as it seems almost immediately after her return home; she died on the 28th of December.

The paper printed Kotoku's letter written to his friend Kosen Sakai soon after her call on him in the cell; in part he writes:

"I should have felt more easy if she had cried on seeing me here. I was awe-struck with the shrill of her old soul heightening to silence. Dear mother was trembling. Silence was a far greater reproach than tears. It is said that the mother always loves the more stupid child, and I know how much she loves me. Oh, how I love her!"

The news was broken to him in court by the lawyer Isobé; his face turned pale, the paper says, for a while, with no word. Then he said in a slow voice: "That is better."

I was instantly moved to tears when I read it, although my senses were somewhat hardened lately; how glad I was, a moment later, to hear Kotoku's heart-cry, sad of course but true! I often ask myself how much of Japanese life is reality; it may not be altogether Orientalism to say that there is nothing real except the fact of love between mother and son. I would venture to say that Kotoku too might be only a little bundle of flesh with an adventurous turn of mind like a thousand others hastening from shadow to shadow, if he had not impressed my mind memorably with that reality of his true heart as he did by accident.

Besides, I had another story in my mind, over which I often cried since my boyhood days, when I took the news of Kotoku's mother so closely to my heart; it is about my uncle who died some thirty years ago, being then younger than I am today. He was a Buddhist priest and poet, Daishun Ukai by name.

I MOST GLADLY GO BACK to the story of my own uncle of heroic temperament natural for a priest of his own age, as if I were an animal who chews back what he ate before, when I feel myself a victim of platitude; the blood on my mother's side, thank heaven, must have been quite ambitious. The talk about him (oh, how I wish I had seen him even once!) I had, a month ago, with the Rev. Hojun Takeda, my uncle's younger brother in faith, now the Father of Komyoji at Kamakura, has still over my thought the same effect as of a red afterglow of a hot summer day beneath which the world assumes a romantic aspect. As the incense arose, the breezes passed away. The Rev. Takeda proceeded:

"I was alone in the temple, that is Jennoji of Ishiki Village, but expecting the Father to be back as he had only gone to the next village. It was almost evening when the village 'dog' (the name given for a detective in those days) called at the temple; he begged permission to let his gentlemen guests from Nagoya rest for while in some room. I consented to it as he was known to me already; the men, two in number, who followed after Shota—that was the name of the village 'dog'—had no peculiarity either in look or speech to incite my suspicion. As usual, I offered them cups of tea and cakes.

"'Tis the most delicious tea,' one of them said. 'Was it brought from Yedo?' The pronunciation of Tokyo for the new capital was not ready on our lips yet in those days. I said to him: 'My brother priest brought it home from there a week ago.' 'Mr. Daishun Ukai has returned, I presume,' the other exclaimed. 'Where is he today? We have had, we confess, much desire to be acquainted with him; his fame as a poet and Chinese calligrapher is widely known in town.' My innocent head, already twenty-one years old then, did not, however, suspect the real nature of those people; and how could I know what secrecy of plot or treason Daishun's bosom had sheltered. It seems that he tried to make his silence cover up the reason of his sudden return after a journey of three hundred miles on horseback; I thought his face was not clear, and he acted strangely restless as if his mind were all stuffed with a matter that could not be revealed before the people prominent socially as well as politically, to whom Daishun always accompanied me. I think now that he soon gave up his hope of raising soldiers from his native province for his plot, with Tatsuwo Kumoi as a leader, that most wonderful rebellious soul, to overthrow the Government newly formed after the completion of the so-called Grand Restoration; and in fact, he had left the temple two days before. Even while I was talking with those visitors, he must have been at your native home in Tsushima. I told them that he had started to Isé Province, and would likely stay at Kounji Temple of Yokkaichi. They begged me to let them look round the temple and garden; after making such an inappropriate apology, they examined every corner of the temple, I might say, even the ashes under the kitchen pot.

"The Father, the Rev. Setsuwo Ukai, your grand-uncle as you know, of course uncle to Daishun, reached home after those suspicious visitors had left the temple. I was telling him about them at length; Shota hurried back again, half an hour later, to assure us that Daishun had surely gone to Yokkaichi, and to reveal the affair in general, most grave as we soon found it was. Shota almost frightened the Father by saying that Kumoi and nearly all of his followers had been already arrested at Yedo, and there was no possible way for Daishun to escape his fate. 'My nephew,' said the Father, 'of whose manly behaviour I have often been proud, would not run and hide himself; you have only to go to Kounji Temple with the city detectives, and meet him, and explain to him about the situation he must accept, and patiently await his surrender. You must remember that he was this Ukai's nephew. Deal with him as a man but not as a common criminal! Don't forget he was my proud nephew!' I believe that Shota and his fellow-detectives started toward Isé Province immediately that evening."

My uncle stopped over night at my home, that is Tsushima, before he turned his face toward Yokkaichi; it is said that my mother, who expected him to appear as a holy priest in black robe, with a golden scarf over his shoulder, was perfectly taken aback on seeing him as a man who had returned to secular life, with hair grown long, unlike a priest, wearing a coat with the dragon crest, that was doubtless Tatsuwo Kumoi's. Kumoi's name was already known to my mother, as it was my uncle who had suggested to her that she might marry Kumoi, who promised him, it is said, to welcome her even without seeing her, and said that the fact of her being a younger sister to him was enough recommendation; but she married my father instead, who passes today as an honest man of the town, now in his seventieth year. My mother was wondering what devil had taken hold of uncle, my mother of deeply religious faith; and now seeing him wear Kumoi's coat, it was quite natural for her to guess how related he stood with him. My uncle, extremely ambitious in his boy's days, was only glad to walk three hundred miles to Yedo for study, as it was the day of no railroad; and when he came of age he was appointed superintendent of the Mitsuun Ryo (a sort of dormitory for priests) belonging to great Zojoji Temple. It is beyond the imagination of the present Japanese what a mighty power that particular temple had; a hundred small temples waited on Zojoji like vassals; the bells were rung and the candles burned day and night; a thousand priests swarmed at Shiba. There were many *ryos* or halls, one of which was uncle's Mitsuun Ryo, the Dense Cloud Hall; it was said that those halls, like many others, had hidden money which was used to accommodate the impoverished lords and *samurais* who were obliged to keep a decent front proper for their standing. And Mitsuun Ryo was one of the richest. I do not know clearly how my uncle became acquainted with Kumoi from Yonezawa; it may have happened that he sought a temporary shelter in uncle's ryo as those priest-halls were a suitable rendezvous for the souls discontented and romantic, mostly sympathetic with the Tokugawa family, looking for chances to overthrow the government the southern people had formed, themselves men who, like Kumoi, hailed from the North; and the priests like my uncle, independent and learned, must have been their splendid companions. It seems that my uncle's poetical turn of mind found immediately the most congenial spirit in Kumoi, whose fame as a poet with Byronic fire is still sung among the students of today. Kumoi wrote one of the very famous ballads for my uncle when he bade him farewell before he started for home: how my young blood used to boil in singing that song, as in the song my uncle must have been quite audacious and strong in temperament. Besides there was, I believe, some monetary relation between them, as I see not a few letters written by Kumoi begging my uncle for a loan; it should be understood that the gold he had would very likely belong to the hall he superintended. One of the most interesting letters that remain in my hand tells that he was afraid to bring guns and cartridges into the hall in the daytime lest it should inspire general suspicion; I am sure that my uncle had a considerable hand in the now so-called Kumoi revolt. He was only in his twenty-seventh year.

The scene changes now from Tsushima to Yokkaichi. He was surprised, when he was leaving Kounji Temple at evening for a walk, to be addressed by Shota from behind, who said that his two friends from Nagoya were waiting at a certain tea-house to make uncle's acquaintance; and he followed Shota as he led him. The fellows who were said to be from Nagoya—of course the same men who had called on Zennoji Temple twenty-four hours before—were drinking *saké*. Without any formal salutation, both of them raised their cups on seeing uncle enter the room, and entreated him to drink, as if he were a friend of thirty years' standing. He had a good taste in wine himself; without pressing to ask them a question about the nature of their invitation, he accepted their offer, and began to drink in a sort of abandon. Did he suspect them? Of course he did. He felt on the spot, when he saw them, that his fate was already sealed. The night grew late; he rose suddenly, and was on the point of leaving them, when they, those detectives from Nagoya, threw over him a long rope that they had hidden most wonderfully under their sleeves. The Rev. Daishun Ukai, my great uncle, looked back and laughed, and said: "I thought you were gentlemen." The detectives, I am told, apologised humbly for their shabby conduct. My uncle begged a grace of half an hour to fix his belongings that he had left at the temple; and as he had promised, he surrendered himself to them gently when the time was up. And he was sent under guard to the prison at Nagoya at once.

Daishun's mother, my dear grandmother, whose sweet memory has yet to be told, was terribly dejected when the news of her son's temporary imprisonment at Nagoya, and the general rumour that she must now prepare for his death, reached her; but when she gained slowly a strength from her conviction that he had done no cowardly crime, although it might not be admirable in all ways round, and that at least it was manly and romantic, her motherly love of a countrywoman, simple and straight, only feared if he might not be hungry in the cell. The day of Daishun's departure for Yedo was announced; my grandmother rose before dawn and filled a large basket with persimmons from the garden, and with the chestnuts she had cooked the night before, and some sort of cake which she thought he would like (it was made, indeed, with her tears). She walked eighteen miles toward Nagoya, and waited for her son's *tomaru kago* or palanquin to pass, under the pine forest by the country road a little off Nagoya, at the place generally known as Kasa Dera, as there the Kwannon goddess wearing a bamboo hat stands. The autumnal sun began to sink; her senses, like the trees and grasses turned gold in the falling light, were perfectly numbed in anxiety and tears. I can well believe that she was almost blind when the palanquin approached like a ghost looming out of mist; her eyesight at once returned with the greatest pain when she saw right before herself, within a palanquin, her very son joining his hands in appeal of pardon, with his face toward his mother. She stumbled forward, bursting into tears, and practically checked the procession. The guards with two swords, more that fifteen, examined her, but her expression of mother's love inspired sympathy in their cold hearts. It is said that even a kind word was spoken to her by them; and her basket was promised to be given to the prisoner. She did not know how she returned home; and she cried and cried over the white palanquin, which was the acknowledged sign of death in those days. But, in fact, it was blue.

He escaped capital punishment from the reason of his being a priest, as a special mitigation was given to the priestfolk; his religious work was worthy of note after his serving a long imprisonment. It is said when he died suddenly in his thirty-third year, that his writing of three hundred pieces of Chinese four-line poems in one night was the main cause of his death. The book of his poems will be published presently; the selection of phrases to be carved on the monument which is soon going to be put up has been entrusted to my hand.

I do not know exactly what was the true motive of his treason; the acknowledged history of the earliest Meiji period only contains two or three lines in vague indifference. And the fact that I did not know him with my living eye, as he died when I was merely four or five years old, only helps to make him shadowy and unreal. But whenever I think of his joining his hands toward his mother in appeal of pardon from his palanquin, he becomes most strikingly a man of reality, all tender and human.

Oh, where is the thing more real than the love between mother and son? "Here lies the son who loved at least his own mother" is the line that might be carved on his tomb.

X

The Lantern Carnival

The evening that flowed out from the forests of Tado Mountain already besieged the valley, in whose shade Tsushima, a town of a few thousand people, laid her soul and body to rest and prayer, when my train dropped me there quite informally some ten years ago. My mind was all uneasy with my rising joy, as it was my first return home after more than ten years of Western life. At the station I frightened my old father; he looked so happy when he made sure that I was his son, real and true—not the foreigner whom he took me for at first. "We must go straight," he said, in a tone that I could not oppose, "to the shrine, and report to the god your safe return. How glad am I that my prayer has been thus answered!" Although I wished in my heart of hearts to see my aged mother first, I could not but obey him, and followed toward the sacred ground. He told me on the way how he lighted a sacred lantern every night for my welfare, and that he had never missed even one day, during those long years of my absence, to pay the god a visit of devotion. It seemed he thought that all my health, all my success, whatever it were, should be attributed to the divine help of the god—I had no quarrel with him about it, of course—and by the god he meant Gozu Tenno, of Tsushima, classically speaking, the Town of Purple Waves. I felt awe-struck, even ashamed, to think that I had neglected to look back to the town god with thanks during many, many years when I stepped into the grounds where the sad loneliness moved like mists, and the holy watch-fire woke the darkness now and then to flight, and the burning lanterns swung as if they were stray ghosts. My old sense of reverence towards this particular god, whom I was taught to revere since my earliest childhood—for I was born here at Tsushima—suddenly returned, and I thought that again the rise and fall of my own life was in his grasp. And how thankful I was for his mercy and divine will!

When I reached home my father lighted those little stone lanterns of the garden dedicated to the god, that is, Gozu Tenno, or the Ox-Head Emperor, "Susanowo no Mikoto" in the Japanese mythology, younger brother to Amaterasu Omikami, Goddess of the Sun. The yellow flame flickered, throwing an uncertain shadow in the room where I slept. Before I wholly fell asleep my mind was moved to compare the cities of the West, where I had spent an ephemeral life, as a bird does from branch to branch, to this Tsushima, the town loved by the god, where the people lead a life of simplicity, which is almost religious austerity. My soul, stricken by the winds and dusty turmoil of the Western life, seemed at once to be healed by the mystery and peace of the town which, in spring, is seen reposing upon a yellow mat of rape flowers, and in summer, is magic with the beauty of lotus. Who does not love his old home? Although I was called soon again to leave the town after this short visit, it became my habit to return home at least once in two years and renew my old association with the Saya River, winding like a silver-sheened snake through the sands, with the pine trees lining the dyke called Saruwo, projecting into the Tennogawa Pond, where the annual Lantern Carnival is held on July 15, of course under the august command of Gozu Tenno.

It is, in truth, one of the wonderful sights of the world, this Lantern Carnival, when six festival cars, each capped by a semicircle of a thousand brilliantly lighted lanterns, make an all-night revel; the thought of them takes me back off-hand to the merriment of my boyhood days. The town would hardly find subsistence if she were not connected with this famous god, known all over the eight provinces of Middle Japan, for she really exists by the pilgrims, although she serves, on the other hand, as a market-place for the people from ten miles round. Indeed, there is no month when the town people do not feel grateful to the god; but when you know that the Lantern Carnival draws more than fifty thousand people with no advertisement whatever, it will be understood that at least half the town makes the greater part of the year's earning in those few days of the festival. It is worth seeing, and not less worth telling to others.

I used to play a flute, with the other children, for our car, which belonged to our street—that is, Nakajima Cho. The six cars are all decorated differently for the day Carnival on July 16, with wax figures from the "No" drama—like Takasago, or the "Old Man and Woman, the Pine Tree Spirits," Katanakaji, or the "Holy Swordsmith," and others—on top, under a wooden frame, with a special roof, the bodies of the cars being covered by gorgeous draperies. It was our work, now twenty or more years ago, to make the plum-blossoms with thin red and white paper for the decoration of the car. How glad we were to engage in the work, ever fired with the ambition to compete with the children of other streets in our skill. And also the work of lighting the candles was entrusted to our hands. The children, as in any other Japanese festival, are the masters of the occasion; they are doubtless the friends of the god. To revive my old association with Gozu Tenno, the patron god of our town, which had become estranged, and, above all, to use the opportunity of returning to my boyhood days, at least in spirit, I decided to leave Tokyo and turn my head homeward on the early morning of July 15 of this year. The sky was clear, as if perfectly wiped; the day was hot. I was happy in my anticipation of the riot of merriment and the beauty of lanterns of the night.

I was told by my mother, when I reached home, that Haru Chan, our neighbour's sweet little son of four years old, had been elected a Chigo, or "divine child," to become the commander of the car for our Nakajima Cho Street. Is not the idea of selecting a child for such an honour beautiful? Let me say, again, that, as this is the god's festival, the children are first in his sacred thought. It is quite a distinction to the child, of course, and also to the family; they treat him with a great reverence, proper to a divine child, as he has ceased to be their own son and has become the god ever since he was appointed to become the Chigo for the festival. A special eating-table, new chopsticks, and new rice bowls will be given him; perhaps a new dress also. It is not out of keeping that they imagine they see the god's presence in their boy's tumbling body. I had no chance to become a Chigo myself, but my eldest brother had. When I was a boy the family storeroom was my haunt of joy, where I used to bring out a little black-lacquered chair and a tiny golden sword, which might be taken for something an angel had loctt but, in fact, were the chair and sword my brother wore as the Chigo on that night half a century ago. I was so amused to sit on that chair with much studied dignity, holding that ridiculous sword and imagining the feeling which my brother must have had as the true Chigo. Oh, Haru Chan, if he can remember the feeling of tonight when he grows old! His innocent little face was powdered; his dress was made of brocade of red and green; he looked quite dignified when he was announced to start leading the procession towards the festival car upon the water. You would never believe, when you see the people in ancient court costume as the servants of honour, that some of them are, in naked reality, mere carpenters, blacksmiths, or itinerant jacks-of-all-trades; but, if a child may become a god, I do not see why workingmen cannot turn to courtiers.

When I approached the Carnival place, that is, the Tennogawa Pond, the roads were completely blocked by the people in merriment and gaiety—in the well-acknowledged mood we call *bureiko*, "of no etiquette." I managed, after much difficulty, to reach our wooden stand, temporarily built on the bank for the family use, when the tops of those six lighted cars were seen through the forest of the said Saruwo, the other side of the pond being their starting-point. By the way, the bank of the pond is one mile long, and not even an inch of space was left by the stands and crowds of spectators, who were prepared to stay awake all night or to sleep in their places. Gozu Tenno, the famous Ox-Head Emperor, makes his august presence this night at the head of the pond, and dominates the festival, of course, with the voice of silence, which we well understand, as we are the people of Tsushima.

Oh, why do the myriad stars fall like rain when there is no wind to blow? They are the fireworks that have burst in the sky. Oh, what thunders are those we hear on the earth when the sky is clear? They are shouts of joy and revelry of the people gathered here. When the cars left the Saruwo, our ears were deafened by the flutes and drums. Oh, where is the sad spirit of night tonight? I am lost to find where is the darkness when the lights of a million lanterns blaze in the sky and turn the waters red. Where in another country can such a night Carnival be found? Even in Japan, only Tsushima, the town of the god, has this distinction; and that town is my native town.

I do not know when the festival cars finished their course on the water under the favour of the god, as I left my stand before it had become very late in the night; and when I appeared again next morning at the stand, I found that those six cars, dressed entirely anew for the day festival, were beginning their slow march as on the night before, but under the sunlight, among the spectators of leaping hearts.

What does all this mean? Although I do not know exactly what it means, I know this: "One is happy with the god in his heart; and a town will be prosperous and full of joy where the god dwells. Such is this Tsushima, the town protected by Gozu Tenno, the Ox-Head Emperor, my own dear native home."

XI

A Japanese Temple of Silence

The room where I am writing—(a while ago the temple bell rang, "trembling in its thousand ages")—is twenty-four mats large, with a high ceiling, unusual to a common Japanese house. It is in a temple; the room is softened into a mellow silence, through which the lonely aspirant can enter into the real heart of Buddhism. The temple, by the way, is Zoroku An, or Tortoise Temple. That is quite a good name for a temple, since a tortoise, it is said, is a symbol of the six virtues of modesty or shyness. On the *tokonoma* of the room I see hanging a large scroll with the picture of Dharuma, the ancient Hindoo monk who established the Zen, this religion of silence. He is represented, as usual, in meditation, his large eyes opened, extremely solemn; it is said that he sat still against a wall for nine long years before he arose with his religion. I once wrote upon this picture of Dharuma:

> *"Oh, magic of meditation, witchery of silence,—*
> *Language for which secret has no power!*
> *Oh, vastness of the soul of night and death,*
> *Where time and pains cease to exist!"*

The room seems almost holy when I think that I can sit before the inextinguishable lamp of Faith, and seek the road of emancipation and poetry, it is here where, indeed, criticism vainly attempts to enter for arguing and denying. And I once wrote:

"The silence is whole and perfect, and makes your wizard life powerless; your true friendship with the ghosts and the beautiful will soon be established. You have to abandon yourself to the beautiful only to create the absolute beauty and grandeur that makes this our human world look trifling, hardly worth troubling about; it is the magical house of Faith where the real echo of the oldest song still vibrates with the newest wonder, and even a simple little thought, once under the touch of imagination, grows more splendrous than art, more beautiful than life."

To get the real silence, means to make imagination swell to its full swing. Through imagination I wish to go back to the age of emotion and true love, when the reality of the external world ceases to be a standard, and you yourself will be a revelation, therefore a great art itself, of hope and passion which will never fail. You might look through the open doors of my room in this Tortoise Temple; you then would see facing you a great forest of Japanese cedars, by whose shadows the Zen monks young or old will now and then be seen as spirits moving on the road of mystery. On the monk I once wrote:

> "He is a pseudonym of the universal consciousness,
> A person lonesome from concentration.
> He is possessed of Nature's instinct,
> And burns white as a flame;
> For him mortality and accident of life
> No longer exist,
> But only the silence and the soul of prayer."

With this entering into the Temple of Silence, I dare say, my third spiritual awakening was well begun. You might ask now, what was, then, my first awakening. It was when I left San Francisco, a year after my arrival in California, in my nineteenth year, and went to the home of Joaquin Miller, an eccentric American bard. There I stayed some three years. *Seen and Unseen: Monologue of a Homeless Snail* came from my first retreat into dream and poetry, the world of silence where is no breath or speech, but the aloneness that is the soul of Nature. I awoke spiritually for a second time in London some eight or nine years later, when I found that poetry and art were the great force of life. I think I was not so sure of making poetry my life's work till I published *From the Eastern Sea*, because New York greatly stole away my precious literary dream of younger days. Now I am glad that I awoke for a third time from sleep with a book of poems entitled *The Pilgrimage* at the Temple where, as I once wrote:

> "Across the song of night and moon,
> (Oh perfume of perfumes!)
> My soul, as a wind
> Whose heart's too full to sing,
> Only roams astray. . ."

Let me recollect how I spent my first night there; that is now almost three years ago.

In the desolation of the Temple of Silence, Enkakuji of famous Kamakura, that Completely Awakened Temple, under the blessing of dusk; it is at evening that the temple tragically soars into the magnificence of loneliness under a chill air stirred up from mountain and glade by the roll of the evening bell. I had journeyed from Tokyo, that hive of noise, here to read a page or two of the whole language of silence, which, far from mocking you with all sorts of interrogation marks, soothes you with the song of prayer. In truth, I came here to confess how little is our human intellect. I slowly climbed the steps, and passed by many a *tatchu* temple like Shorei An, Zoroku An, and others, which serve as vassals to great Enkakuji, and finally reached the priest-hall to learn, to my no small delight, that the opening ceremony of *Dai Setshin*, or "Great Meeting with Spirit," was going to be held that very night.

For the priests of this Zen sect, to which Enkakuji belongs, the year is divided into four parts, each called a *ge*, which is three months. And the two *ges* running from August 15 to October 15, and from February 15 to May 15, called *Gekan* or *Seikan*, meaning "Excused from Rule," are the months of freedom for the *dai–shu*, as we call the priests, while they have strictly to observe every ascetic rule during the other two *ges*. We call the latter "Within the Rule," or *Seichu*. And the most important time during the *Seichus* is the week of *Dai Setshin*, which falls three times during the period from May 15 to August 15. Now, as this was the 14th of May, I was to have an opportunity of being present at the opening ceremony of the "Great Meeting with Spirit," which I had wished to attend for some long time.

The hall was not yet lighted, as it was a little before seven o'clock (that is the time of "candles lighted"), when I quietly crept into it like a wandering breeze seeking the soul of Nirvana. And I was at once conducted by a young priest into the Assembly Chamber. I say he was a young man, but who knows whether he were not an old priest?

It seemed to me that I was already led into a magic atmosphere, in whose world-old incense—what a song of exclamation!—I lost all sense of time and place. Here the silence-wrapped monks seemed to my eyes as if they had returned long since to those grey elements of nature which stand above Life and Death. And it is the very problem of Life and Death you have to solve with the Zen philosophy, if you like to call it philosophy.

The chamber, although it was quite dark already, could be seen to be wider than fifty mats; and here and there I observed that the *kojis* or laymen were taking their appointed places, doubtless communing in their souls with that Silence which does not awe you, but to which you have to submit yourself without challenge, with a prayer. Silence is not here a weapon as it might be in some other place; it is a gospel whose unwritten words can be read through the virtue of self-forgetting.

I was gracefully entering into dream, which is a path of retreat into the world of silence, when a priest brought into the chamber the lighted candles, announcing that the ceremony would soon begin. Straight before me was a candle whose yellow flame rose in the shape of hands folded in prayer to the Buddhist image, which I could observe behind the lattice door of the holy dais of the chamber. What a face of profundity, which is but mystery! And that mystery will become at once the soul of simplicity, which is nature. I was told that the Buddha was nobody but the right mind, to whom the perfect assimilation with great nature is emancipation, and that you and I can be the Buddha right on the spot. It is the dignity of this Zen Buddhism to arise from devotion, pity, love, and the like; it is not a religion born in your understanding, perhaps, but the highest state of mind before yourself was born, breaking the peace of the world. You have to leave your human knowledge before you may enter here. And so did I, to the best of my ability.

The *hangi* or wooden block was tapped, and the monks, fifty in all, slipped into the chamber from another independent house called the "Meditation House," shaven-headed, black-robed spectres from the abyss of night. They muttered the holy name, and then sat down in a row by the *shojis*. A moment later a coughing voice was heard without, and then the sound of straw slippers moving on the pavement. I looked back, and saw three *bonboris* (paper-shaded hand candlesticks) floating forward, and then the figures of four priests. The chief priest, who lives in a house on the other side, was coming, led by his attendants. The silence of the chamber was deepened when they slipped in and took their own places.

The chief priest sat before the lattice door of the Buddha image shrine. He was a man of sixty, heavily built, and sleepy looking, doubtless from his saturation in silence; he wore a robe of yellowish-brown colour, with a large scarf of old brocade across his shoulder.

He looked around and said "*Hai!*" We laymen with all the priests bent our heads upon the mats, and kept them so, while the chief priests finished the reading of Shogaku Kokushi's words of warning:

"We have three classes of students. One who casts away every affinity with fire, and studies his own self, is the very best. There is one whose practice is not so particularly pure, but he loves to learn; he is in the middle class. One who quenches his own spiritual light and delights in licking the Buddha's saliva is of the lowest. If there be one who drinks only the beauty of books, and lives by writing, we call him a shaven-headed layman, and he cannot be in even the lowest class of our students. (How despicable is one who writes for writing's sake!) And, of course, we cannot admit into our Buddhist circle one who spends his time dissolutely eating and sleeping too fully; the ancient worthies used to call such an one a clothes-horse and a rice-bag. He is not a priest at all, and cannot be allowed to enter the temple-grounds as a student; indeed, even his temporary visit cannot be permitted, and of course he cannot beg to stay here with us. Thus I say; but you must not regard me as one who lacks sympathy or love. I only wish our students to find out their wrong and correct their faults, so as to become a seed and shoot of Buddhism, and so grow."

Then the chief priest said:

"There is no dream which is not born from the bosom of reality; and we have no reality which does not sing of dream. You may call our life a dream if you will; there is no harm either to think of it as a reality. The main point is that you have to arise from the dream and the reality of life, and, let me say, from life itself. You must not be fettered by life; death is nothing but another phase of nature, and we hear another harmony of beauty and music in it as in life. Let the pine tree be green, and the roses red. We have to observe the mystery of every existence, human or non-human; these do not challenge but submit to one another, and complete the truth of the universe. To connect mystery with our Zen Buddhism does it no justice. There is no mystery whatever in the world; and truth which may appear to an unclean mind to be a secret, is simplicity itself, which is the soul of nature and Buddha. To attain to the state of Buddha through the virtue of meditation whose word is silence, is our salvation. The language of silence cannot be understood by the way of reason, but by the power of impulse, which is abstraction. Sakyamuni, it is said, picked a flower, which he showed to all the priests who gathered at Reizan Kaijo; all of them were silent, but Kayo Sonja smiled. That smile is the truth of self-possession and deliverance; we long for it."

All the priests stood and read the "Dharani of Great Mercy," and ended with their vows of consecration:

"We vow to save all innumerous mankind;
We vow to cut down all the exhaustless lusts;
We vow to learn all the boundless laws;
We vow to complete all the peerless understanding."

Then the tea was poured in our cups and some parched rice slightly sugared was served out on pieces of paper which we carried. (It is the temple's rule not to trouble another's hand.) We drank the tea and ate the rice. Then the chief priest rose and departed in silence, accompanied by his three attendant priests as before. When their steps became inaudible in the silence of the night, and their *bonboris* disappeared in the bosom of darkness, all the priests rose and retired to their Meditation House, and I to the guest-room next to the Assembly Chamber, conducted thither by one of the *fuzuis* or under-secretaries of this priest-hall, who left with me a piece of writing. It read:

"Rising: two o'clock A.M.
Prayer: three o'clock.
Breakfast: four o'clock.
Offering to the Buddha: eight o'clock.
Prayer: nine o'clock.
Dinner: ten o'clock.
Morning-bell struck: eleven o'clock.
Lecture: one o'clock P.M.
Prayer: half-past two o'clock.
Supper: four o'clock.
Evening bell struck: twenty minutes past six o'clock.
Prayer: seven o'clock.
Sleep: eight o'clock."

The room in which I found myself had all the desolation of the senses which scorns the flame of excitement—(the subduing of excitement is the first principle here)—that I had found in the Assembly Chamber. I felt the silence deepening, when I perceived I had nobody, not even a priest silent as a ghost, near me. Now and then the hooting of an owl searched my ear from the mountain at the back; and the candle burned lonesomely as my own solitary soul.

Some time ago I had heard the *hangi* struck announcing the time to put lights out and go to sleep. But I am sure there is many a priest who

YONE NOGUCHI

will meditate all night sitting up in the darkness; the darkness for him will be the Buddha's light to lead him into the silence of conception.

I tried but in vain to go to sleep, then my own soul—whatever it was—became more awakened. I read the words written on a *kakemono* hung on the *tokonoma:* "Hear the voice of thy hand." It must be one of those questions of which I have heard, put by the chief priest to the monks, to be answered through their own understanding. Here we must find our own salvation by the power of our contemplation. . . Where is the voice of your hand except in yourself? And, again, where is the truth except in your own soul? To understand your own self is to understand the truth. The voice of truth is the voice of your own hand. I raised my head toward the *shoji;* through its broken paper I caught sight of a star in the profundity of silence. "Silence is emancipation," I cried.

I could not rise at two o'clock next morning, as I had wished; and I felt ashamed to be called by a priest to leave my bed and get up for breakfast. When I made my appearance in the Assembly Chamber, which was a dining-room in turn, all the monks were already seated, silently and even solemnly, as on the previous evening. They muttered a short prayer before they brought out their bowls and chopsticks from under their black robes. (They are their only belongings, beside one or two sacred books.) With them I had the severest breakfast that ever I ate; it consisted only of some gruel, chiefly of barley, with a little rice as an apology, with a few slices of vegetables dipped in salted water. However, I enjoyed it, as they did.

I thought their diet was far beyond simplicity, while I admitted their pride of high thinking. And I wondered if it was true asceticism to abandon every human longing, so as to make the way clear for spiritual exaltation, for flying in the air as a bird, and not walking like any other animal. It is written, I am told, in the holy book, of the dignity of poverty, that it should be guarded as sacred law. (Oh, to think of the luxuries of the West!) These priests are sent out begging far and near every month. Begging is regarded as divine, a gift as the expression of sacrifice and self-immolation. They live on charity. They do not beg for the sake of begging, but to keep the spirit of the Buddha's law; then there is no begging. Meikei of Toganowo, the Buddhist teacher of Yasutoki Hojo, the Hojo feudal prince, was asked to accept a great piece of land of the Tanba province for his temple expenses; but he refused with many thanks, saying that there was no greater enemy than luxury for priests, who, under its mockery, might become dissolute and cease to observe the holy law. "Mighty Poverty, I pray unto thy dignity to protect Buddhism from spiritual ruin," he exclaimed. Such is the Zen's loftiness. I remember somebody said that he could pray better when he was hungry. I read the following "list of charity receipts" in the office of the *fusu* or chief secretary:

> "Ten yen for the great feast.
> Ten yen for Prajña-reading.
> Eight yen for the general feasting.
> Four yen for feasting.
> Three yen and a half for lunch-giving.
> Three yen for gruel-giving.
> Two yen and a half for rice-giving as a side-dish.
> Seventy sen for cake-giving.
> Thirty sen for bath-giving."

No woman is privileged to enter the priest-hall; here the monks themselves wash, cook, and sew. The four priests under the Tenzu Ryo take upon themselves the cook's responsibilities; the Densu priests attend to cleaning the dais and images. And there are the two priests at the Jisha Ryo who serve Monju Bosatsu, the holy image enshrined in the Meditation House; here they offer tea and bowls of rice at the proper time. Those who look after the vegetables are called Yenju; and there are three attendant priests on the chief priest. The chief secretary with his two assistants manages the whole business of the priest-hall.

This Enkakuji embraces mountainous ground of some five hundred acres, where, in the olden days when we had more devotion, more than forty small temples used to stand, but today only twenty of them survive the accidental destruction of fire or natural ruin. By the way, the priest-hall belongs to Seizoku An, one of the *tachu* temples. Enkakuji was founded by Tokimune Hojo, hero of the Hojo feudal government, who cut off the heads of the envoys of Kublai Khan at Tatsunokuchi, and then destroyed the Mogul armies on the Tsukushi seas. He was a great believer in Zen Buddhism, and on its power he nourished his wonderful spirit of conviction and bravery which triumphed in Japan's first battle with the foreign invasion some six hundred years ago. And it was the Chinese priest called Sogen Zenji whom he invited here to this Enkakuji, and to whom he made his student's obeisance. Indeed, here where I walk in the silence under the twittering of birds from the temple-eaves, through the sentinel-straight cedar trees, is the very place. Here he exchanged confidence and faith with mountains and stars. He must have sat, too, in the Meditation House, just as those fifty priests whom we see sitting there today. In truth, *zazen*, or sitting in abstraction, is the way to concentrate and intensify your mind so that it will never be alarmed, even amid the crash of thunder or at the sight of mountains falling before your eyes.

You have to bend your right leg and set it in the crotch of your left, which, too, must be put on your right. Then the back of your right hand must be placed on the left leg, and the back of your left hand within your right palm; and both of your thumbs must be raised to form a circle. You must not look up nor down; your ears and shoulders must be straight in line, and also your nose and navel. Open your eyes as usual, and breathe in and out slowly. Above all, you must find the place of imaginary existence of your soul right in your left palm. Then will your mind grow into silence, as Buddha on the lotus-flower—how pure the silence of that flower—floating on the peaceful bosom of the universe, pure from all the sense of life and death, you and nature being perfectly at one. Silence is the power of nature; it is the true state in which to perfect one's existence. It is non-action—which does not mean inactivity; it is the full urge of active actionlessness. It is the very completion of one's health and spirit.

Our forefathers thought it a matter of great pride to die right before their master's horse in battle; they thought, as one saying goes, that to die was to return home. Life for them was a temporary exile which should not be taken too seriously. They respected frugality as a virtue; they did not think that speech was a proper defence, and entrenched themselves in the language of silence. The temple of silence, such as Enkakuji and others, was for them an indispensable shrine of spiritual education. Here at Kamakura they found their proper sanctuaries.

Enkakuji was burned down three or four times by the warriors' fire, all of it except one little temple, called Shari Den, beside the Meditation House, where some particles of Buddha's bones, some part of his jawbone, it is said, are enshrined. I could well believe that even the hearts of boorish warriors were melted by the warmth of Buddha's glory. Shari Den is a small affair of thirty-six feet square, crowned with a thatched roof. As perfect harmony with nature, not only spiritually but also physically, is the keynote of Zen Buddhism, the aged soft, dark-brown colour of thatch was preferred—the colour of submission and contentment. This small Shari Den is now under the government's protection as a model structure of the Zen sect temples of the Kamakura period which followed the So style of China. The second gate of the temple enclosure, that mass of structure of two stories, carrying all the weariness and silence of ages in its colouring, is a giant of surprise which, however, does not amaze you unduly; but the magnificent aspect of its massive dignity will make you really wonder whether there may not be a certain power of spirit shining through its ashen surface, by which it still makes manifest its immensity of grandeur. Not only the gate, but many other things about the grounds seem soaring beyond the grasp of ruin; I dare say they will continue to exist indefinitely by the power of prayer and silence. Indeed, this is the ground of mystery, however the Zen may deny it. You will learn, I am sure, that carvings, gargoyles, dragons and the like, are not everything even for a Japanese temple. And what a grandeur of simplicity! Let us learn here the grey simplicity of truth!

A somewhat squat building of a similar character of structure to that of the gate-tower, some fifteen ken square (one ken is six feet), will receive you after the gate, if you wish to offer your prayer. Prayer is the "Great Clear Shining Treasure" of your mind, as the tablet carved from the autograph of the Emperor Gokogen, which you see above the doors, has it. The floor is paved with the lichen-green squares of tiles which add their tragic emphasis to the already twilight soul of the edifice. Strangely gesticulating incense is seen rising from the altar toward Sakyamuni, colossal, gold-robed, and with a gold crown, who is companioned by two lonely figures of guardian Bosatsus. This is the place where, by virtue of your prayer, you can forget your human speech, and rise on high into the light of silence. If only one could stay here till the blessed day of the Miroku—the expected Messiah, whom the Buddha promised to give us after the lapse of five thousand years!

I walked slowly in the temple grounds, and again and again thought over what I had read of Zen Buddhism. And I repeated:

"The law of the world and man, for sage as well as for common folk, should not be forced to be understood; let it be as it is. It is neither difficult nor easy. To take it as it is, in truth, is the real understanding. Drink tea when you are thirsty, eat food in your hunger. Rise with dawn, and sleep when the sun sets. But your trouble will begin when you let desire act freely; you have to soar above all personal desire. You may be far away from the real law when you first determine to reach the perfect understanding; but not to be perplexed with your doubt is the right road, whereby to enter into the true perception. We have no reality, neither goodness nor badness; we create them only by our own will. Separate yourself from love and hatred, or be not fettered with love and hatred; then the real law shall reveal itself clearly. The law is one only, but it expresses itself in a thousand different forms. Here are mountain, river, flower, grass; the moon, sun, are not the same things. But the law which makes them to appear for their existence is the same law. To one who understands the law's true meaning, they are the same thing, or the same thing under different forms. The law is eternal; its power covers the whole world. And yet if you are blinded with your own self, you cannot see it at all. We call it disease of soul to have love fighting with hatred, goodness with badness; and if you do not understand the real state of the law, your silence will be foolishly disturbed. To gain the perfect silence, this is victory; it makes you soar high above your self and doubt. Silence is the expression of the real law of the world and man. By its virtue you can join perfectly with great Nature. Then are you Eternity itself, and you are Buddha."

To make the separate self to cease from its selfishness is the keynote of the Zen. After all, it is nothing but the religion of universal love and humanity.

XII

Epilogue

Charles Warren Stoddard

I HAVE WRITTEN QUITE MANY of my own stories; but still many more are left unwritten. I have been thinking for some long while that I shall go minutely in recording my own memories of my childhood days; and I must say something about my dear father, who died the most ideal death in his seventieth year last July (1913), surrounded by his five children and others. The readers will find somewhere in this book the name of Isamu, a boy from my first marriage; but I said nothing about Hifumi, Haruwo, and Masawo, these three children whom the present wife of mine, a Japanese, brought to me. I am sure that the stories about them will furnish me another book.

Here is one man, now dead, by the name of Charles Warren Stoddard, whose memory I cherish in my inner heart; I cannot leave out his name from the present book. He was the author of *South Sea Idylls*, the book loved by Stevenson; he himself was one of Stevenson's friends. Stoddard has a charming essay or memoir of this great romanticist in his *Exits and Entrances*. Richard Le Gallienne once invited us, Stoddard and I, for dinner in his little roof-garden in New York city; that was in 1904. And it was almost the last time when I was with Stoddard. Many a lantern was lighted that evening. There was a young man in the party who had been telling me of his breezy experiences in the South Sea; Stoddard's eyes eagerly followed the moon while listening to the story. What a sweet moon-night it was! His soul, I am sure, must have been cruising in his beloved coral seas—severed from every tie, politely letting the world slip by. The teller of the story assured us that the foreign missionary and the American tipping custom were speedily spoiling the whole island.

"They are a nation of warriors and lovers falling like the leaf, but unlike it, with no followers in the new season," Stoddard sighed.

Then soon after this memorial night, he left New York for good as he said; he went to Boston, and then to California. It was in the last place where he died several years ago by the song of the ocean whom he loved passionately. I had written an article on him in some American magazine in 1904 from which I like to quote the following:

So, our love (love between Stoddard and me, by Buddha's name) was sealed one spring day, 1897. Sweet spring usually bringing a basketful of some sort of surprise! I climbed up the hill—those days I spent with Joaquin Miller, loitering among the roses and carnations—and threw my kisses toward Charley's "Bungalow" in Washington. Eternally dear "Charley" (as he was called in California)! The air was delicious. I gathered all the poppies and buttercups, and put them in a sprinkler. I offered it to my imaginary Charley. From day immemorial he had appeared a sort of saint—a half-saint at least. If he ever accepted my offering!

It rains today, the drops tapping my window-panes frequently. What could be more welcome than the renewal of memory? For some while I have been looking over old letters. How wildly I used to laugh at my grandfather engaging in the same task in my boyhood's days! Here's Max Nordau's. There's a poem written by the genial Professor Van Dyke. This long letter minutely written on the sky-blue sheets should be from my dear William Rossetti. What encouragement he bestowed on me! What pains he took in suggesting a certain change for my poem! Isn't this the acknowledgment of her Majesty, the Queen of England, for my book? Look at the dear little crown in red upon the envelope! That is by a certain Duchess! There is a huge bundle of the letters sent by Charley. What a correspondence! My letters were an avalanche of sorrow usually. Once upon a time I was quite proud in telling of the many griefs in my life. He would begin his letters with "My sad poet." Shall I trace back our love, following the dates? He once addressed me:

"Sometimes at sea, in the midst of the wave arrested wilderness, a weary and affrighted bird falls panting upon the ship's reeling deck.

"It was born in the Garden of Spices; it bathed its wings in perfume; it sang with all the wild, free singers of the grove; at night the stars glinted on its dew-damp plumage, while it slept on its fragrant bough.

"But a fierce wind came and whirled it afar through the empty spaces beyond the sea's grey rim—whirled it afar until it fell panting and affrighted upon the ship's reeling deck.

"Then those who were on board tenderly nursed it, and caressed it, and gave it generous cheer, but the bird ceased its song—or if it sang it sang only of the Garden of Spices, for it was an exile for ever more.

"So thou seemest to me, O Yone! like the weary bird, torn from its blessing bough, and whirled into the midst of the wave-crested wilderness.

"They who have found thee, would comfort and caress thee—I most of all—but thy songs are tear-stained, and thou singest only the song of the exile—a lament for the Garden of Spices, and all the joys that were."

What a disappointment I must be proving myself to him nowadays! "You are a poet of common sense," he denounced me not long ago. Am I practical, I wonder? However, I feel like teasing him once in a while, saying lots of disagreeable things upon his living without setting his feet on the ground of Life—I, playing the part of bee buzzing around a big idol. He will turn his large blue eyes—how pathetically appealing they are—and, of course with a sort of smile, say: "God made me!"

I have been getting rid of the sad muses lately. I whistle into the air. I smile up to the sun. Didn't he plan, some time ago, to fly from the world—he with me—and bury ourselves in some obscurity (somewhere where he could smell the roses abundantly and keep a few intimate books and "a parrot to swear for fun")?

I found myself in the East first in 1899. Ho, ho, Washington, Charley's Bungalow! Till that day we had embraced each other only in a letter.

I couldn't imagine his "Bungalow" without the ivy vines, some of which would venture in through a broken window—the broken window adding a deal of charm. Yes, there they were. How I wished it were not so modernised with the door bell! A door knob if you must. There the moon would crawl from the eastern window into the library, as if a tired spirit (tired is Charley's) peeping into the pages of a book. What a tremendous number of books—each book with the author's sentiments in autograph! Certainly a few tassels of cobwebs wouldn't be out of place.

"O Yone, you would fit in there," Charley exclaimed. We both sat in one huge chair with a deep hollow, where we could doze comfortably, its long arms appearing but a pair of oars carrying us into the isle of dream. It would have been more natural had I been barefooted and in a Japanese kimono. "You are far too Westernised," he condemned me terribly. He looked at me critically and said: "How handsomely you are dressed, Yone!" Did he expect me to be another Kana Ana—a little sea-god of his South Sea, shaking the spray from his forehead like a porpoise? (What charmingly lazy *South Sea Idylls* by the way!) I am positive he prayed that I would come to him in some Japanese robe at the least.

We talked on many things far and near—things without beginning and apparently without end. We agreed upon every point. We aroused ourselves to such a height of enthusiasm. He told me a thousand little secrets. (Aren't little secrets cosy?) Is there any more delicious thing than to listen to his talk about nothing? Sweet nothing! The nothing would turn to a silver-buskined anecdote at once when it was told in the Bungalow—especially by him. What a soothingly balmy atmosphere in the house, which might have been blowing from a forgotten book of poems! How full of little stories he is! "Dad," I exclaimed. It was only natural for me to say that.

We slept in the same bed, Charley and I. Awakening in the night I observed that a light in the holy-water font, a large crimson heart—now isn't that like Charley's?—was burning in golden flames like a baby's tiny hands in prayer. What a solitude, yet what sweetness! It wouldn't be strange if we became a sort of spirits in spite of ourselves. By my side the dear Charley was sleeping like a tired faun. Should I cover his head with the ivy? Occasionally he snored, as if by way of apology for his still keeping this life. (Thy life be eternal!) I saw a scapular around his neck, and a tattoo of the sacred cross on his arm, done in Jerusalem—how romantically Rome sounded to him! He is a Catholic. He cherished such a sort of thing with child's devotion. I wonder if I ever came across any more simple man than himself. He just reminded me of the Abbé Constantin in the novel of Halévy. (What a dear book is that!) I shouldn't be surprised to see him any day, counting a rosary, with downcast eyes, around a monastery—San Francisco del Deserto, perhaps. I left the bed. I prayed for his happiness.

Poor old Stoddard! His lovely writing—what a breeze, what a scent in it!—didn't succeed in bringing him an ample livelihood. He has been always to the edge of that success which he has never reached. It is an eternal question whether pure literature will pay. "If I could only write trash!" he would exclaim.

He had been in the South Sea to shake off the world's trouble. He had returned to civilisation again, perhaps after turning to a half-savage. How he wished to be a barbarian, and live for ever in some cosy spot! There would be nothing jollier than to eat with one's fingers, using a leaf for a platter. He is always puzzling to find out where he belongs. Not in America, to be sure.

"Yes, sea-chanting beach of Lahina, or under the banana leaves of Tahiti! By Jove, if I could return over there! I could build such a life as here we can only dream of," he would say, flashing a sort of dreaming eyes. He had been longing with abundant lamentation, like one after the wife he has divorced.

It would be that he couldn't grasp tight the real meaning of life, if he were a failure itself, as he says. He is a born dreamer. He has been living in the world without any motive. (It may be just the opposite, although so it does appear.) He doesn't know any worldly routine. There is nothing more welcome to him than writing. He will often answer, however, with something about his "pen-fright," when some editor asks for an article on a certain subject. He would begin to look unhappy since morning, if it were his lecturing day. He was professor in the Catholic University, Washington, District of Columbia. It was not so much on account of the work. How he hates to be constrained! He wishes to be perfectly free. After all, he is nothing but a spoiled child. "I am even a baby," he will proclaim off-hand.

He will serenely fill a convenient corner and "look natural," and perhaps think about sweet nothing, and occasionally get very solemn— that is all he likes to do. Do you know how he fits such a pose?

He was in New York last June. He appeared like an abandoned boat—perhaps a Hawaiian canoe—terribly tottering on the ocean waves, not knowing whither he was going.

(I often thought he was a genius who had sprung up in the least advantageous time and place. What a wonder if he should prove himself under the right shade!)

"'Tis my life—my whole history of failure! I feel shame in such a clear exposition of myself," he cried one day, holding his *For the Pleasure of His Company*, which had then been published from San Francisco.

"I am sure you would like Miss Juno," he reflected a moment later, speaking of one of the characters in his book.

Doubtless he must have fallen in love with women in his life. He might have married one of them if he had been sure of not getting tired of her after a while. He often said, how could he ever forget the scar of a wound which he might give her in saying or doing something he ought not to say or do—something that would make her hate him.

"I am a born coward," he would say, if you denounced his having no blood to risk.

THE END

A Note About the Author

Yone Noguchi (1875–1947) was a Japanese poet, novelist, and critic who wrote in both English and Japanese. Born in Tsushima, he studied the works of Thomas Carlyle and Herbert Spencer at Keio University in Tokyo, where he also practiced Zen and wrote haiku. In 1893, he moved to San Francisco and began working at a newspaper established by Japanese exiles. Under the tutelage of Joaquin Miller, an Oakland-based writer and outdoorsman, Noguchi came into his own as a poet. He published two collections in 1897 before moving to New York via Chicago. In 1901, he published *The American Diary of a Japanese Girl*, his debut novel. Noguchi soon tired of America, however, and sailed to England where he published a third book of poems and made connections with such writers as William Butler Yeats and Thomas Hardy. Reinvigorated and determined to continue his career, he returned to New York in 1903, but left for Japan the following year following the end of his marriage to journalist and educator Léonie Gilmour, with whom he had a son. As the Russo-Japanese War brought his nation onto the world stage, Noguchi became known as a literary critic for the *Japan Times* and focused on advising such Western playwrights as Yeats to study the classical Noh drama. He spent the second decade of the century as a prominent international lecturer, mainly in Europe and Britain. In 1920, Noguchi published *Japanese Hokkus*, a collection of short poems, before turning his attention to Japanese-language verse. As Japan moved closer toward war with the West, Noguchi turned from leftist politics to the nationalism supported by his country's leaders, straining his relationship with Bengali poet Rabindranath Tagore and distancing himself from his former colleagues around the world. In 1945, his home in Tokyo was destroyed in the devastating American firebombing of the city; he died only two years later, having reconnected with his son Isamu.

A Note from the Publisher

Spanning many genres, from non-fiction essays to literature classics to children's books and lyric poetry, Mint Edition books showcase the master works of our time in a modern new package. The text is freshly typeset, is clean and easy to read, and features a new note about the author in each volume. Many books also include exclusive new introductory material. Every book boasts a striking new cover, which makes it as appropriate for collecting as it is for gift giving. Mint Edition books are only printed when a reader orders them, so natural resources are not wasted. We're proud that our books are never manufactured in excess and exist only in the exact quantity they need to be read and enjoyed. To learn more and view our library, go to minteditionbooks.com

bookfinity & MINT EDITIONS

Enjoy more of your favorite classics with Bookfinity,
a new search and discovery experience for readers.
With Bookfinity, you can discover more vintage
literature for your collection, find your Reader Type,
track books you've read or want to read,
and add reviews to your favorite books.
Visit www.bookfinity.com, and click on
Take the Quiz to get started.

Don't forget to follow us
@bookfinityofficial and @mint_editions